# Analyze This!

## A Teen Guide to Therapy and Getting Help

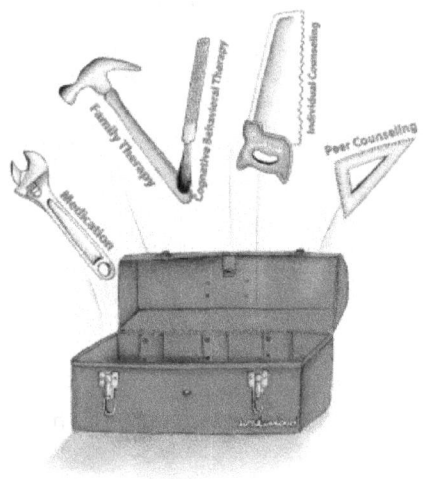

By Youth Communication

Edited by Laura Longhine

# Analyze This!

**EXECUTIVE EDITORS**
Keith Hefner and Laura Longhine

**CONTRIBUTING EDITORS**
Nora McCarthy, Hope Vanderberg, Rachel Blustain, Al Desetta,
Sean Chambers, and Kendra Hurley

**LAYOUT & DESIGN**
Efrain Reyes, Jr. and Jeff Faerber

**COVER ART**
Sara Goldys

Copyright © 2009 by Youth Communication ®

All rights reserved under International and Pan-American Copyright Conventions. Unless otherwise noted, no part of this book may be reproduced, stored in a retrieval system, or transmitted in any form or by any means, electronic, mechanical, photocopying, recording, or otherwise, without express written permission of the publisher, except for brief quotations or critical reviews.

For reprint information, please contact Youth Communication.

ISBN 978-1-933939-85-8

Second, Expanded Edition

Printed in the United States of America

Youth Communication ®
New York, New York
www.youthcomm.org

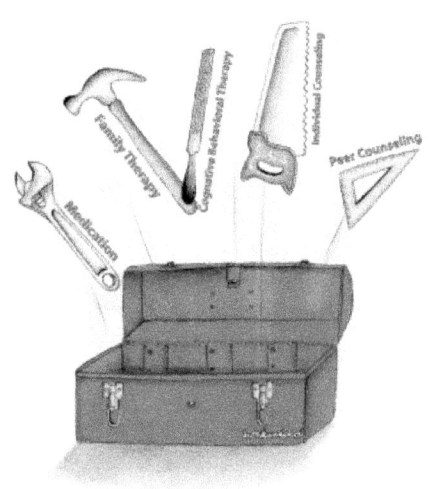

## Table of Contents

Don't Keep It Inside: Talk It Out, *Norman Brant* ........................ 13
    *With his fourth therapist, Norman finally finds someone he can open up to.*

Therapy: What It's All About, *Carolyn Glaser* ........................ 18
    *A therapist briefly describes what to expect.*

Taking Control of My Moods, *Erica Harrigan* ........................ 20
    *Diagnosed with borderline personality disorder, Erica learns to manage her emotions through therapy and medication.*

Get Outta My Head! *Charlene Carter* ........................ 27
    *Charlene explores why foster youth are often resistant to therapy.*

Opening Up, *Natasha Santos* ........................ 30
    *Natasha connects with her latest therapist in a way she never managed in the past.*

Getting Out of the Swamp, *Andrew Starr* ........................ 37
    *Andrew's therapist helps him deal with his anger and sadness about not living with his family.*

My Journey Back From Depression, *Samira Hassan* ........................ 42
    *When Samira is sent to a mental hospital, she feels trapped until a sympathetic social worker helps her open up.*

## Contents

Worried Sick, *Megan Cohen* ..................................................................... 48
    *Megan has always been an obsessive thinker and worrier, but when her anxiety threatens her friendships, she decides to consult a psychologist for advice.*

Explaining Cognitive-Behavioral Therapy, *La'Quesha Barner* ... 53
    *La'Quesha learns about a kind of therapy, that helps people change their behavior by changing how they think about it.*

A Shy Girl Finds Her Voice, *Mayra Sierra* ........................................ 57
    *Mayra is skeptical about participating in music therapy, but the program helps her express her feelings.*

Listening to My Inner Child, *Aquellah Mahdi* .................................. 62
    *In art therapy, Aquella creates a doll that stands for her "inner child"—and allows her to express childhood feelings that she's kept hidden.*

Learning to Forgive, *Christopher B.* ..................................................... 67
    *Christopher begins to forgive his mom, and they start family therapy together.*

Family Therapy: A Safe Place to Connect ........................................... 73
    *How family therapy can help parents and kids reconnect.*

Searching for Dr. Right, *Maya Noy* ...................................................... 76
    *Maya has been in therapy for years, but has had a hard time finding a therapist she feels comfortable with.*

## Contents

How Therapy Changed My Life, *Anonymous* .................................. 82
*At a youth shelter, the author gets connected with a good therapist who helps him release his anger.*

A Hard Pill to Swallow, *Gloria Williams* .................................. 88
*Gloria enjoys therapy until she's switched to a therapist she doesn't like and is put on medication that makes her feel like a "lab animal."*

What Are Anti-Depressants? *Carolyn Glaser* .................................. 94

Inside a Psychiatrist's Head, *Gloria Williams* .................................. 96
*A psychiatrist talks about the pros and cons of medication.*

Crazy for Psychology, *Erica Pierre* .................................. 99
*Erica decides that she wants to become a psycologist, but her family thinks that's crazy.*

The Therapy Stigma, *Erica Pierre* .................................. 104
*Erica interviews psychiatrist Alvin Poussaint about why therapy has a bad name.*

Walking Away From the Fight, *Anonymous* .................................. 107
*The writer turns to therapy when she can no longer handle her father's rage.*

FICTION SPECIAL: Lost and Found, *Anne Schraff* .................................. 115

## Contents

A Teen Guide to Getting Help .................................................. 124

Mental Health Terms You May Want to Know ...................... 134

Teens: How to Get More Out of This Book ............................. 138

How to Use This Book in Staff Training ................................. 139

Teachers and Staff: How to Use This Book In Groups .......... 140

Credits ........................................................................................ 142

About Youth Communication ................................................. 143

About the Editors ...................................................................... 146

More Helpful Books from Youth Communication ................ 148

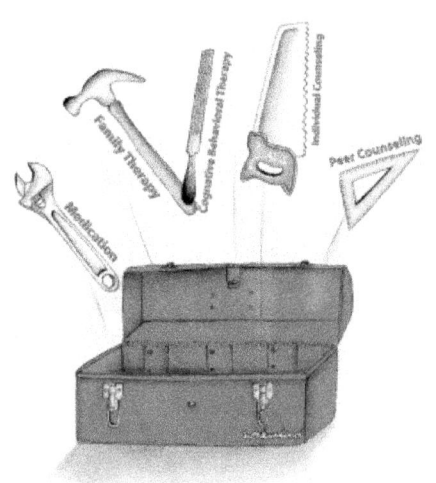

# Introduction

Many teens struggle with difficult emotions like sadness, anger, anxiety, or depression. Some also suffer from more serious problems, like severe depression or other mental illnesses, substance abuse, cutting, or eating disorders. Therapy can provide a supportive place for teens to talk about these feelings and issues and find ways to start feeling better. But too often, adults send young people to therapy without taking the time to explain how it works or how to make the most of it. As a result, while many teens are happy with the help they are getting from therapy or medication, others are dissatisfied, angry, or confused.

In this book, teens write about their experiences with therapy and therapists—the good, the bad, and the in-between. Their stories show what therapy can and can't do, what good therapy looks like, and what it takes to make it work. At the end of the book, our "Teen Guide to Getting Help" explains the options teens have for dealing with emotional problems, and how they cang get the kind of help that works best for them.

Some teens have a negative view of therapy because they were mandated to go, rather than being able to make the decision themselves. As Charlene Carter says about teens in foster care: "Their experiences with the psychiatrists and therapists are often bad simply because they don't want to be there in the first place." Other writers get turned off to therapy through bad experiences with therapists who can't relate to them.

Whenever the teens in this book have found therapy helpful, they almost always describe a therapist who they were able to connect with, someone respectful, straightforward, and caring, someone "real."

In "Talk It Out," Norman Brant goes through multiple therapists who "just skimmed the surface of the problems" before he finds a therapist who can help him. Here's how he describes that therapist, Dr. K:

"She didn't talk to me like I was a toddler. And she hardly ever talked about herself. She didn't act like I had to take her advice just because she went to school for it. And if I ever forgot to come for an appointment, she'd call to remind me. That alone made me feel like she really cared."

When teens are able to open up to therapists they trust, they often find a great sense of relief. Andrew Starr writes that talking with his therapist, Ted, helps calm him down and relieve his stress. After Aquellah Mahdi opens up about feelings from her past, she experiences "a feeling of inner peace." And for Christopher B., being able to release his anger toward his mother in therapy allows him to start forgiving her. When he and his mother go to family therapy together, they learn to communicate in a new way.

At its best, therapy is not only a relief valve, but a place where teens figure out how to deal with stressful situations, and how to change their behavior in ways that help them feel more satisfied and capable of reaching their goals.

Through a combination of therapy and medication, Erica Harrigan, who suffers from borderline personality disorder, is better able to control her moods and avoid emotional outbursts. After building up her confidence with a therapist, Mayra Sierra starts to express herself to her mother, which makes her feel less afraid. And the author of "Walking Away From the Fight" turns to therapy when she's overwhelmed by her difficult father. She learns that while she can't stop him from lashing out, she can find different ways to respond, to defuse arguments and feel more calm.

"Therapy isn't magic," she concludes. "It doesn't necessarily make things better for you; it gives you the tools to make things better for yourself."

---

*In some stories, names have been changed.*

# Don't Keep It Inside: Talk It Out

### By Norman Brant

In the past four years, I've had four different therapists. Each time I went to one I was hoping to find someone who cared enough to tell me the things I did wrong and help me go about changing them. But until I found my fourth therapist, I was lost inside my own world.

I went to my first therapist at age 12. At the time, my life was filled with chaos, and I didn't know who to talk to or how to handle it.

My dad was in jail, my mother and I weren't talking, and in a little more than a year, several family members had died. All the feelings I had began to build up inside, and I felt like I was drowning in my emotions.

Sometimes I would cry like a baby over all the death in my

# Analyze This!

family. Other times I'd feel angry and confused. I didn't trust anyone, especially my family, and I thought people were saying negative things about me. I started to disrespect my elders, steal, stay out late, and fail in school.

Things got so bad that I was sent to two different group homes. At the homes I pretended to feel better about myself, but being there made me feel like more of a failure and like I didn't deserve to live. I really needed someone to talk to. I needed someone to show me that there was still hope for me and to help me realize that everything that was going on wasn't all my fault.

I went to one therapist after another. But my therapists didn't ask how I was really feeling, which was what I wanted. Instead they just skimmed the surface of the problems and offered me useless advice like, "Watch your temper," or "Try to fit in."

But my fourth therapist, Dr. Kaputer, was different. She didn't talk to me like I was a toddler. And she hardly ever talked about herself. She didn't act like I had to take her advice just because she went to school for it. And if I ever forgot to come for an appointment, she'd call to remind me. That alone made me feel like she really cared. Slowly I began to open up and tell her more about myself.

I remember one time I was hit in the face by another resident of my group home, and it left a mark under my eye. From that day until the mark went away, I was picked on. It was like I was garbage in a dumpster, and the residents were the seagulls—just picking and picking at me until there was practically nothing there.

I pretended that what they said didn't hurt, but it did. They would say things like "Norm's a punk," or "Check out big Norm with the black eye." Even though it was a joke to them, it wasn't to me.

At first I didn't want to talk to Dr. K about the fight. I didn't care how it started, or the consequences I had to suffer. It was the reactions I got from people that bothered me, and that was what

I wanted to talk about.

She asked me how I felt about all the attention I was getting. Of course I said I was angry and didn't like it. But then she repeated the question, explaining that she wanted to know how I really felt about people making fun of me.

Again I tried to work my way around the question, but I didn't get far because she asked again. Finally, I told her, "It hurts so bad until I can't describe it," which is what she wanted to hear—and what I needed to say. How I really felt. After that session, it became easier for me to express my true feelings.

Another time someone spread a rumor saying that I had sex with one of the residents. That whole thing went around the entire campus infecting people's brains like crack. And it lasted for weeks.

***I needed someone to help me realize that everything that was going on wasn't all my fault.***

Some of the residents would say, "Your roommate said you had sex with another resident," or "Yo, I heard you was gay, is that true?"

To me, that was hurtful and embarrassing. I felt like I wanted to die, but I never let anyone know how I was really feeling. I just made myself go completely numb to the hurt, only feeling anger. But it didn't work because all my other feelings continued to build up, colliding and swarming around like the winds of an unpredictable storm.

I was rude to the other residents for the littlest things. Like when one asked if he could have some of my cereal, I responded, "No, what the hell do I look like giving you something of mine, anyway?" He just rolled his eyes and walked away.

Another resident asked if I had a bar of soap he could borrow. I said, "Do I look like your freakin' mother to you?" He just started mumbling and walked away, too.

My anger was a reflection of how much I was hurting inside. Because I was hurting so badly and didn't want anyone to know,

# Analyze This!

I became more and more angry, and that's when Dr. K really got down to business.

She told me she thought I was trying to get at people's most sensitive, vulnerable sides, so I could make them feel the way I felt. Then she began to dig deeper.

Instead of just telling me not to act out anymore, she asked me why I did it. How did it make me feel to insult someone? Did I think it was a positive thing to do?

> **Dr. K. didn't act like I had to take her advice just because she went to school for it.**

At first I didn't know what to say to her questions because they were so direct. I explained to her that the things they said about me really hurt. And it wasn't just the fact that they weren't true. It was the fact that some of the same people saying these things claimed to be my friends.

But I also liked that she was willing to be so direct with me. With questions like that, I knew we were getting somewhere and that I was dealing with someone who cared. Which is what I wanted all along—someone who was going to be there whenever I needed her. Someone who understood both sides of the story.

Working with Dr. K, I learned not to get so angry at so many little things. She helped me uncover a side of myself I never knew I had and showed me how to look at myself from the outside in. With her help, I realized that the ways I was acting were just a cover for my true feelings.

I still have to work on expressing my feelings more and not always thinking someone is talking badly about me. I still have to work on watching the things I say or at least how I say them. Which may take a while.

But Dr. K also helped me see that the things that went on at my group home weren't all my fault, and what was my fault I'd have to admit to. And Dr. K helped me realize that I actually did have a reason to live.

Dr. K helped me beyond words. She was the only person I trusted. So it really hurt me the day I found out she was leaving. I just felt like shutting out everything around me.

It's going to be hard to start with another therapist because I don't feel like going back and talking about my past after doing it with four other therapists. I just want to move forward.

I just need someone I feel I can trust, with whom I can really talk about myself and my life. Sometimes, I just need to talk about me. Just me.

---

*The author was 16 when he wrote this story.*

# Therapy: What It's All About
## (In 250 Words or Less)

### By Carolyn Glaser

In therapy, people have the chance to talk about what's going on in their lives. They also have a chance to discuss what's affected them in the past, as well as how the past affects what they're thinking and feeling now.

Therapy is not supposed to make you the happiest person in the world or make you perfect. It's supposed to make you feel good about who you are and help you live your life to your full ability. It's supposed to help you learn to be competent and deal with hardships, because life is hard.

---

*Carolyn Glaser is a therapist at The Door,*
*a multi-service teen center in New York City.*

Sometimes people start therapy thinking they're going to feel better immediately, but they usually feel worse before they feel better. That can last a month, or several months, because therapy is digging, and you're often digging up painful stuff.

It's also important to have the right therapist. Just because a therapist is great doesn't mean he or she is the right therapist for you. Sometimes you just don't click. It's important to be able to say, "I don't like this, it's not working for me." The therapist should be able to see it too and switch you to someone else if it's not working.

In therapy, confidentiality is very important. The only time that should be broken is when someone threatens to kill themselves or someone else. Other than that, your therapist should be the one person you talk to who's not going to tell anyone your business. If you don't feel safe, it doesn't work.

# Taking Control of My Moods

### By Erica Harrigan

I was sent to get a psychiatric evaluation last year, at the request of the family court. At the psychiatrist's office, I sat in a black chair and began to bite my nails, thinking about what to say and what not to say to the doctor. I was afraid that if I said anything that made me look loony I'd be leaving there in an ambulance to the nut house. I stopped biting my nails when the psychiatrist stepped into the room.

He asked questions about my childhood experiences, personal information that I've been trying to block out because I don't want to remember. It was like opening up the gate to hell in my brain.

I have written about those childhood experiences—being beaten and neglected at home, raped, and locked up in a psychiatric hospital for two years. Writing gave me a sense of closure about the memories. For the psychiatrist to ask me to bring up my childhood experiences again made me feel like my brain was burning inside.

I answered each question the best I could without losing it. I talked at a fast pace and in a high voice, alert to my reactions. I have limited patience and staying there long would have triggered my angry side. I can get violent and harmful when I become angry. I didn't want to attack the psychiatrist.

He had a little book that he was checking things off in every time I answered a question. It was a book to determine if I had a mental illness. About a week later I received an evaluation in the mail. It said I have Borderline Personality Disorder (BPD) and explained that therapy and medication could help.

I looked up borderline on the internet and found out it is a serious illness that creates powerful mood changes. Typical symptoms include anxiety, distress, lack of confidence, and mania. I read that borderline can interfere with interpersonal relationships, self-image, work, and an individual's sense of dignity. The illness may lead to suicide attempts, weird thoughts, and many hospitalizations.

Those descriptions fit me to a T. I switch in a heartbeat from manic happiness to impulsive aggression and self-injury. I saw myself when I read that "people with BPD often have highly unstable patterns of social relationships. They develop intense but stormy attachments. Their attitudes towards family, friends, and loved ones may suddenly shift from enormous respect and love to intense anger and dislike."

***I was afraid that if I said anything that made me look loony I'd be leaving there in an ambulance to the nut house.***

Those descriptions of borderline also scared me. I thought, "After all I have gone through, now this?" Being labeled made me feel like I didn't know myself, like I was a stranger in my own body. I knew I had trouble with my feelings switching up, but I hadn't taken it seriously. Come to find out I don't have all my screws in my head.

I was relieved when I read, "Mental health services can eventually help a person with borderline live a productive life."

But then I saw that on my evaluation, the psychiatrist wrote that I should see a therapist, and that medicine might help but not much. There is no way to change my personality. The medication can only help slow down my moods so they're not changing abruptly.

Soon after I got the evaluation, I began therapy. My therapist was a young woman who was not yet fully a therapist. My first impression was not good. I thought, "This is a wanna-be therapist from college who figured she'd like to play pretend." First impressions are not a good way to judge, I know now. My therapist turned out to be cool peoples.

Sometimes during my visits I felt like I was in the hot seat, because all the attention was focused on me and my issues. But it didn't bother me to tell her about my feelings and experiences. It felt as if my therapist was reaching out to help me, not like she just wanted to get paid and didn't care what I'd gone through.

One thing I really liked was that she had flexible hours and days. She didn't cut my conversation short because of time. Sometimes we stayed past the time limit. She also allowed me to come more than once a week when I was feeling down or when I was excited to tell her something and felt I just couldn't wait until my session.

My therapist and I talked at first about how I ended up with such a serious condition. She said some people believe borderline is the result of negative experiences and others say it's just your chemical make-up. I assume it's both. Both my mom and dad have moods that change quickly, from loving mother to depressed mom or angry mom and from loving father to angry dad.

At first, my therapist and I just talked about things I wasn't upset about at the moment. We paid attention to my behavior and moods outside the office and found out that I end up having emotional collapses when I have a small negative experience and don't deal with it right away. As my hurt builds into anger, I start to feel like I'm not in control of my body anymore, and my behavior becomes intense. I learned that I can help myself manage my outbursts by opening up and letting out my feelings in positive ways.

During most of my early appointments, I was smiling and calm. Then one day I was feeling suicidal and I was honest with her about it. She really helped.

I was feeling suicidal because my ex-boyfriend was treating me badly. He often borrowed money from me that he didn't pay back, and he wasn't faithful. I had broken up with him, giving him his Christmas gift and telling him, "Merry Christmas, but I'm at my new boyfriend's house." After that he got angry. He kept calling me, arguing and hanging up, expecting me to come back to him.

I felt upset because he'd hurt my feelings while we were dating but he wouldn't admit that I'd hurt him at all. He just kept saying, "I don't need you. It's best that we break up. I only need you for your money." I believed that, once again, I'd opened my heart to someone who didn't care about me. Jerk!

**I was relieved when I read, "Mental health services can eventually help a person with borderline live a productive life."**

I wanted him to suffer and felt suicidal because I thought I'd never find someone to love me without hurting me. Weep! Weep! I actually started sharpening my knife with the back of a can opener, even though I knew I didn't want to hurt myself. I was feeling blue and wanted attention. I know pulling suicide attempts is not a positive way to seek attention, but I decided to act out my thoughts anyway. I felt out of control and wanted to be rescued. Sometimes I show people how I am feeling and pray they can help me. My new boyfriend stopped me in my tracks.

The next morning I called my therapist and she asked me to come in. I was relieved. Any other therapist would have sent me to the nut house. I went right to her office.

She was surprised to see me so upset. I felt a little weird that she saw me in the middle of flipping out, and I worried that she'd see me differently after that. But she's treated me the same.

Like always, she told me to take time alone to myself in the corner of her room. She asked me to answer questions, like, "What could you have done instead of wanting to commit suicide?" And, "What could have happened if you did go through with it?"

I sat in the corner and thought about my ex-boyfriend, good times as well as bad. I realized that I didn't need him. Over the past year dating him all I felt was pain. Love is supposed to bring joyful moments in life.

After a little while I thought, "I don't know what I was thinking!" I told her, "I could have called a friend, spoken to staff, or talked to my boyfriend."

"Great!" she replied. She went over ways for me to get help if I ever felt like harming myself again, like calling a 24/7 hotline number, her number, or if it's serious calling 911.

We also talked about my wish to be rescued. I learned that it will help me to think, "How can I help myself?" more often than, "How can someone help me?" I can help myself in many cases (although I can become lost-minded and act in strange ways at times).

When I left the therapist's office I felt brand new, like I'd stepped through a warm tunnel filled with happiness. I was smiling and happy to be alive. I thought, "Boyfriends come and go. I was thinking about hurting myself over a stupid situation."

What made me feel better wasn't really anything she said,

but what she pulled out of me. Her questions helped me put into words solutions that I had inside all along. I was blinded by my emotions, but in reality I was glad the relationship was over.

I've learned a lot from therapy. We've talked about so many things. I learned that I have an addictive nature. I'm addicted to friends and men who treat me badly and I want everyone to like me. I also compulsively buy stuff in shops that I never had but always wanted as a child. My therapist and I decided that an addiction isn't easy to get rid of 1-2-3! It takes time. I try to handle each problem step by step.

My therapist and I also started a "Forgive and Forget" plan because I have trouble keeping a distance from people that hurt me in the past. She told me to call everybody and tell them, "I forgive you," and to forgive myself, too.

I called a friend I once fought with. He'd called me names and I'd insulted him back. When I called, I said, "I want to end this like adults, not little children. I forgive you and I hope you forgive me."

> **Her questions helped me put into words solutions that I had inside all along.**

I also wrote letters to my mother and father. I told them that while I had issues with them in the past, I know it's a hard thing to raise children and I know they did the best they could and I forgive them.

Both of my parents wrote back and told me they were proud of me. My mom also told me that she'd been through some of the same pain as me (she'd been raped as a child, too) and my father told me that he was struggling with his anger problems. Their words made me feel like some of the pain from my past that I haven't been able to let go of is starting to fade.

I also started taking new medications a few months ago to stabilize my moods. The medication is to help me be the kind and caring side of myself, not the side that gets mean and nasty towards people. At first I felt that being on medications was the most awful part of my illness. But I've found that it's better taking medication than being unstable.

I'm so glad I got that evaluation and went to therapy. My therapist is more than a therapist. She lends an ear, she gives me practical help and she is like the friend I always wanted.

I have improved my ability to express myself with words instead of acting out my feelings. I have more improvements to make. But at least now I can stop when I get angry and tell myself, "Think! Think of all the ways you could react, and react in a positive way."

As a result of attending therapy I do feel much better. She didn't cure my illness, but she helped me have many more positive days than I had before.

---

*The writer was 20 when she wrote this story.*
*She later married, had two children,*
*and trained as a home health aide.*

# Get Outta My Head!

### By Charlene Carter

"Just because you're mandated to go to therapy does not mean you have to sit there and let the therapist enter your life."

This is what Sarah Beth Frishman, a therapist in New York City, said about kids in foster care who are required to go to therapy. I was talking to her about therapy because often kids in foster care are forced to get psychiatric evaluations. Their experiences with the psychiatrists and therapists are often bad because they don't want to be there in the first place. And no one has worked to help them learn how to get the most out of therapy. They don't want to go to the many counseling sessions, they don't want to give details about their lives to a stranger, and they don't want to take the medication prescribed for them.

Being told that they have to do those things can make teens feel that they're being manipulated by the foster care system, and that their rights are being abused. Therapy is supposed to help people, but when you don't want to be there and you're forced to go, it can end up making you feel worse.

When I got my psychiatric evaluation and was told to go to therapy, I felt manipulated. I felt that I didn't need to go to therapy at the time. I see this happening in my group home: The residents will go for an evaluation and then become very annoyed when they're told that they must attend therapy. They complain about it, but very little is done to accommodate them. Most of the time they have to go to therapy and, because they don't want to be there, it ends up being a waste of their time and the therapist's time. What is the point of that?

Frishman agreed that if someone in therapy doesn't want to be there, chances are they won't get a lot out of it. "It's difficult to force someone," said Frishman. "Part of therapy is being ready and willing."

People in therapy who want to be helped have to be willing to work with the therapist and to reveal parts of themselves, like their feelings, which can be hard to do. Talking about difficult parts of your life can bring up uncomfortable emotions, like sadness or anger. "When giving out intimate details, hard core data about themselves, kids have different reactions," Frishman said. "Some are ashamed, some surprised, and some don't seem to mind it at all."

Talking through whatever emotions come up, she said, can make someone feel better in the long run. Frishman strongly felt that therapy could be useful to anyone, and especially kids in foster care who have been taken away from their family, which is painful in itself. Therapy can give kids in foster care a safe space to talk about their feelings with an adult who listens, not judges. And it can help those kids better understand themselves and how events in their lives have affected them.

But often kids in foster care are not ready to commit to therapy, regardless of how much it could help. Maybe they feel that whatever they tell the therapist will be told to someone else, like their group home staff. And some of us feel that the time and energy spent in therapy is too much, and distracts us from our other goals, like finishing school or getting reunited with our parents.

This can lead to lots of misunderstandings between group home residents and staff, because the staff expect the kids to abide by the agency rules at all times. In my group home, sometimes a resident faces consequences for refusing to go to therapy. Staff may take away that kid's privileges, like not letting her use the telephone for two days. This can make the resident angry, and that anger can lead to more problems in her life.

*If someone in therapy doesn't want to be there, chances are they won't get a lot out of it.*

Yes, therapy may be able to help some of us. But the staff must realize that if we are not ready and willing to go to therapy, being forced to do it may affect us in many negative ways. And we may start thinking negatively about therapy and therapists in general.

Perhaps all of us in foster care need good therapists who care about us and who will give us the time and space and attention that we need from an adult. Maybe if there were more therapists who really listened to the child and respected her reluctance to share difficult details about her life, then kids in foster care would be more cooperative when it came to going to therapy. But for now, many teens become disappointed when they're forced to go to therapy. Therapy will not be effective for us if we don't want to be there, or if we feel manipulated.

"You can lead a horse to water but you cannot make it drink," Frishman said. That is, if we don't trust the process, chances are it just won't work.

---

*The author was 20 when she wrote this story.*

# Opening Up

**By Natasha Santos**

"So what do you think about that?"

"What do you think I think about that?"

"Well, I think that you're avoiding the question."

For months that was a typical conversation between my therapist and me. Rachel would ask me a question, and I would ask her the question back. I wasn't going to easily give her access into my deepest thoughts. I had been seriously traumatized by bullsh-t therapists before. If this lady wanted to me to trust her, she would have to work for it!

That's exactly what she did. I hated it when she would ask me seemingly obvious questions like, "How do you feel?" and insist that I answer them. I usually wouldn't at first. I'd give her an annoyed look and a blank-eyed stare and hope that she would let the stupid question drop. She never did.

*Opening Up*

I decided to go to therapy when I was 16 because my mother had died, I was having trouble in school and my adopted family wasn't the best at helping me handle my problems. First I went to my school social worker. She encouraged me to go to a therapist. I went to the intake (first session) with my mom, feeling very wary and uncomfortable. I was on the lookout for fake pity and stereotyping therapists.

From ages 9 to 12 I had gone to court-mandated bi-weekly therapy sessions with my last foster mother. She spent 30 minutes telling the therapist I was a liar and a thief and how disgusting I was, and spent the remaining 15 minutes lecturing me about how I could be better and more loved if I would just change. "Just try, that's all we're asking, Tasha," Diane would say with a smug smile on her face. Not really listening, I would nod and smile. My therapist wasn't a very big part of the session. It seemed like she was just there to agree with whatever my foster mother said.

At 14 I returned to the same therapist—and finally realized how clueless she was about my real needs. She was all about dealing with my current problems, like what I had done in school that day or if I'd had an argument with my new foster mother. Her advice felt generic and uncaring. "Talk about it with them" was all she would say. I never did and she never followed-up.

I stopped going to her after several sessions. I didn't say why. I just told everyone that I didn't need therapy. I felt that no one could do me any good. If I needed something I would have to find it someplace else or not at all. If I was feeling sad or upset about something I would go to my older sister, but even that had its limits. I usually ended up in my room crying and sulking until I couldn't pity myself anymore.

Those were very depressing times.

Then my mother died and school troubles followed. About four months after my mother died I was beginning to fail classes. I felt the need to talk, but I didn't have anyone to talk to. My adoptive mother recommended therapy. But I wasn't going to open myself up to that hurt again. Instead I met with the social worker at my high school. When she asked me if I would consider seeing a therapist, I said no.

But after meeting with the social worker a third time (the maximum allowed), I began to consider it. The school social worker listened to me and seemed to care about what I was saying, so maybe her colleagues would be the same way. The school social worker didn't condemn anything I did, but considered—and asked me to consider—the reasons behind my actions and feelings.

So my mom and I went to the intake just to see what it was about. We sat in the waiting room filling out form after form about my personality and what I was there for and my past history in therapy. I was nervous and slightly uncomfortable.

As we sat in the small waiting room, a group of about 20 kids filed out of a corridor and into the street. "You guys have 10 minutes for a smoke break," a woman called to them.

"Maybe this won't be such a bad place after all," I thought with a slight smirk. "What kind of place is so free as to allow teens to take a smoke break?" Unconventional. Good. Conventional therapy hadn't worked for me in the past.

I started seeing Rachel every week. I like Rachel's persistence. She has a calmness about her, which is good in case I ever decide to go completely emotional. One of my biggest fears is that in the midst of dealing with something I'll go all emotional and do something I can't take back. I've told Rachel about my fear, but she doesn't seem too concerned about it.

She wasn't in a rush to get me to the version of myself she thought I should be. Rachel seemed more human to me than any of my shrinks; she liked to talk about clothes, she listened to music and she's even let me borrow a CD or two. Rachel is real in a way none of my other therapists were.

A couple of months into our sessions, Rachel suggested having a session with my adoptive mom. I had been telling her about how my mom and I were having trouble communicating with each other. Rachel felt that we needed a safe place to talk. I was completely against it because of my past experience with my old foster mom. But she was insistent, so within two weeks I was sitting across from Rachel and next to my mom, feeling dreary and acting as bitchy as possible. If they wanted war, they'd get it.

"So Tasha, why are we here today?" Rachel said.

"I don't know, why?" I said, looking at the floor.

"Natasha, if you want us to help you, you're gonna have to communicate with us," Rachel said.

"I don't need this kind of help," I said, reaching for my third piece of chocolate from the candy dish she kept on her bookshelf.

"Why don't you put down the candy and talk to her," my mom said in exasperation.

**If this lady wanted to me to trust her, she would have to work for it!**

I wasn't talking to anyone. I'd been against this meeting from the start, and if it was going to go to hell, I sure wasn't going to waste my breath and energy trying to save it. The session proceeded like that until we left.

My mother exited the room stiff and silent. Rachel seemed severely annoyed. I was oddly pleased with myself. Later that night, at home, I apologized with a smirk on my face and my mother knew it wasn't real so she didn't accept it.

In the next session, Rachel wanted to talk about what had happened. I was interested in her analysis. "You have told me in the past," she said, "that you had been hurt when you had your foster mother in the room. And when you were put into that situation again last week you were saying, 'No! I am not going to do this! Other people have hurt me in this way, and I am not letting you in to do the same thing.'"

"Yeah," I thought, "she got it." Maybe I could trust this one after all.

After six months, I began to open up to her more as I realized that everything we did and spoke about was really on my terms.

# Analyze This!

I wasn't consciously aware that a connection was taking place. I noticed that I was talking more and that I wasn't always dreading the sessions, but I would never admit to trusting her as much as I did. I wasn't sure about how safe my feelings were. Hadn't I allowed other people to get close in this way before, only to get hurt?

Now, after two years, I finally feel comfortable enough to start conversations with her and tell her when I don't agree with her without being rude. I feel like she really cares about what I have to say and I value her opinion as well.

I used to begin a session by telling Rachel to ask me a question. If I liked the question I would answer it, and if I didn't like it I would tell her to ask me another one. Sometimes I didn't want to talk about myself, just what was going on around me or in the world. She never pushed me to talk about myself in every session.

After a while I would freely tell her about what had gone on that day. Soon we were having conversations about Diane (my former foster mother) and the state of black people in America.

Now Rachel and I usually discuss how I've been feeling over the week, and how much of that is from my past experiences and how much of it is a feeling that anyone might have in a similar situation. One time I was telling her about a boy I liked and how afraid I was to approach him. I was mortified that he would say something really mean and self-esteem-destroying to me and I would run home crying.

Rachel asked me how much of my fear came from what I knew about that boy, and how much came from my past experiences living with foster parents and "wanting to be loved and accepted but getting rejection," as she put it.

I eventually came to the conclusion that I hadn't really seen or heard anything that should make me so nervous about approaching him. My fear came from my past. Experience had taught me that if I tried to gain acceptance from someone, they would reject me. (I never approached the guy, though. As is the way of crushes, I was over it in another week.)

Learning how my past experience is affecting my present life has made me more aware of what I think and feel, and more aware of what others may be thinking and feeling. I've become more confident knowing there's more than one way to look at any given situation.

It's taken a long time, but we recently started talking about why I had come there in the first place. It's been a slow process. It's not about how much I trust Rachel but how much I feel ready to deal with.

We haven't gotten around to talking about my mother's death (it's still too painful) but we have spoken about the memories I have of her, good and bad. She hasn't pushed the issue, and I appreciate that.

I eventually changed schools and we spoke about what that meant to me in my educational career and life. I had a feeling of failure and terror similar to the one I'd had when I left Diane's house. We spoke about how a part of me felt that it was essentially my fault Diane didn't want me and that's why I had to leave. And how I felt the same way about my school. We decided that sometimes people and places don't click and that it may not be anyone's fault.

> *I began to open up to her more as I realized that everything we did and spoke about was really on my terms.*

The main thing that we are still working on is my adopted family and my place in it. I was adopted when I was 15 and have found it hard to understand my family, which comes from an entirely different culture. Rachel tries to get me to consider who my mom is and how impossible it is to make someone change.

Just last weekend my mom and I were arguing over the rules in the house and how I should be neater and more respectful of her rules. I felt—and still feel—her rules are unfair and odd. I feel like she wants me to behave like an adult but still treats me like a

# Analyze This!

child. We argued for about an hour until she left.

She hasn't really spoken to me in the past five days and I haven't really had anything to say to her. But I got to thinking last night about how she must feel about me and the place she's had to make for me in her life. Perhaps she's worried that I still don't feel a part of the family, and that I'll start going crazy now that I am 18. Perhaps she's worried that if I haven't learned neatness and respect at 18 then when will I learn it?

I've decided to bring all this up with my mom the next time I see her. Before I met Rachel I probably would never have considered looking at things from my mother's point of view. Rachel taught me to try to see things through others' eyes.

It's a good thing I've done it, too, because I'm only allowed to be in the program until I'm 19. Before I leave, I want to be able to deal with things by thinking them through, and understanding people's limitations. I'm working toward that with Rachel. I feel more confident and safe knowing that I've learned how to think and solve my problems myself.

---

*The author was 18 when she wrote this story. She later worked as an Americorps volunteer and attended the University of New Orleans.*

# Getting Out of the Swamp

**By Andrew Starr**

"You don't want to be stuck in the swamp," my therapist Ted said to me one day as he pointed to a sloppy drawing of a stick person on a curvy line. I must have looked confused because he continued to explain. He told me that, as I go through my life, I will have to face many challenges. Ted said I can face those challenges or I can run away from them.

"When you run, you're taking yourself back to the swamp, and the swamp is not where you want to be," Ted said. "But if you stay focused on accomplishing your goals, you are facing those challenges and you'll eventually win."

Facing the challenges in my life has been the focus of my therapy sessions with Ted. My anger has been the main problem that has gotten me into some very tricky situations, including being placed in a juvenile detention center, getting kicked out of schools and missing many classes. As a result, I am now far behind in my school work and every day is a challenge for me to try to catch up and continue to control my anger. With Ted's help, I think I just might be able to do it.

*I* am 15 years old and I have been in foster care for about six years. In those six years, I have lived in at least 12 foster homes. I started going to therapy the first time when I was 8 or 9 years old because I was depressed about being far away from my family.

It was especially difficult when my mom would say she was coming to see me, and then not show up because she didn't have a ride. Sometimes she'd forget to call and tell me she wasn't coming and that made me even more depressed. I would worry that something had happened to her, and if there was no reason for it I'd feel abandoned by her and all alone.

My social worker at that time thought I needed therapy, and I agreed. I had a lot of sadness to deal with. And I thought, "What could it hurt?"

My first therapist, John, was on staff at the group home where I lived, and he would sometimes help on the unit if they were short-staffed. This was a good way for him to see me interact with peers and get to know me outside of therapy. But it was still hard to know who I could trust after everything that had happened to me. John tried to help me, but we never really connected.

After about a year, John felt that my attitude and behavior had improved, and he recommended that I leave the group home. I think therapy did help a little. It helped me realize that some people do care and everyone isn't as bad as they seem. I'd started to express myself a little more and I got my act together.

But I still found myself opening up my eyes and seeing that, although my depression might have improved somewhat, my issues will never be completely resolved, even after I leave the system. I will never get those years back that I could have had with my family.

About four years later, I was just getting settled into another new foster home. I really needed to talk to someone about my new living situation and about being in the foster care system, period. So I suggested to my foster mom that we get help. My foster mother got a referral from a co-worker for a good African-American therapist, and that's how we met Ted.

What I like about my foster mom is that she was willing to go and discuss some of our problems together, and Ted was always willing to have us. We were hoping to improve our relationship, and therapy helped us do that. Over time, my foster mom and I really grew to love one another. I also started seeing Ted on my own.

> *My social worker thought I needed therapy, and I agreed. I had a lot of sadness to deal with.*

I didn't trust Ted immediately, but it didn't take very long. Ted's funny, and most importantly, I really think he understands what I have been through in my life. I felt at ease talking to him because of our similar backgrounds. He had also been in foster care and he had some of the same problems I had growing up.

I have been meeting once or twice a week with Ted for almost a year now and I feel pretty comfortable talking to him. He helps me think about things in different ways and tries to keep me focused on my goals. Since I started meeting with Ted, we have been working on three major challenges in my life: learning to control my anger, adjusting to new schools and learning to express my feelings through my writing.

I have a lot of anger inside because of being in the system. I've missed out on a lot of time with my family, and I don't even know some of my family members. Ted has told me to release some of my anger by writing in my journal. He has also encouraged me to put pieces of my life into my stories and even poems.

# Analyze This!

Now when I get mad I make up stories to express myself. After I write, I feel relieved, calm and focused on something else. Ted also encourages me to spend time by myself to calm down and then to talk to the person I have a problem with to try to fix whatever's wrong.

Even though Ted talked to me a lot about controlling my anger, he never really got to see what it looks like. Then one day my foster mom dropped me off on the wrong side of the street and that made me very angry. I had to walk in front of a lot of people and I felt stupid because everyone was looking at me.

As I walked up the stairs to Ted's office, I was swearing under my breath. When I looked up, Ted was standing there and he had heard everything I said. He looked shocked and said, "I never thought I'd see the day." We spent the rest of that session talking about how I could have handled the situation better.

*He helps me think about things in different ways and tries to keep me focused on my goals.*

Another big challenge for me has always been going back to school or starting at a new school. I have gone to about 15 different schools and have been in many different kinds of settings—mainstream classes, alternative programs, group homes and resource rooms to name a few.

I don't like to be in big crowds of people and I can be very shy. It's not that easy for me to make friends. Ted is always able to calm me down and help me to stop worrying so much.

This year, I started 9th grade at a big public high school. Ted helped me feel less nervous by telling me that my fears were all in my head. He told me to go to school and stay focused on my goals, and not to worry about what people say or do.

Ted and I mostly talk about whatever is on my mind at the moment. But I think that as the relationship builds, I'll be able to talk to him more about deeper stuff.

Ted addresses problems with me and he always has some

helpful solutions. I always feel better when I talk to him and when I am able to release some of my stress. I trust his judgment, and I believe he actually knows what he's talking about.

Even though Ted has helped me face a lot of challenges, once in a while I still take a trip back to the "swamp." Sometimes, though, when I feel like I'm heading to the swamp, I can hear Ted's voice saying: "Face these challenges and you will succeed." That's exactly what I plan to do.

---

*Andrew was in high school when he wrote this story.*

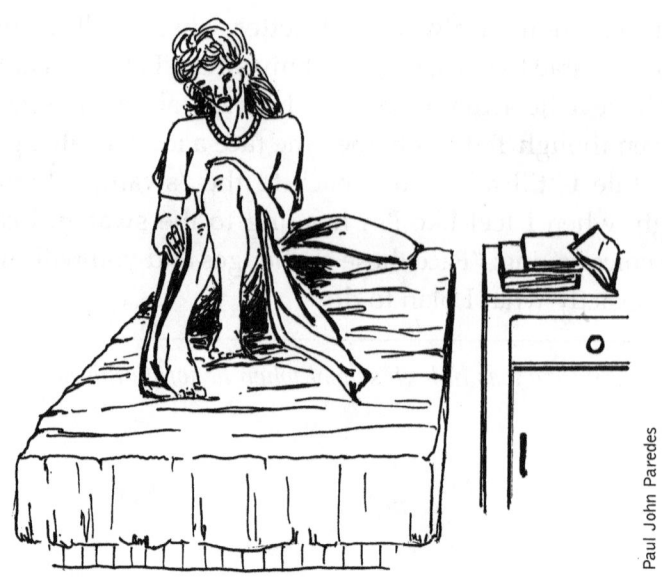

# My Journey Back From Depression

### By Samira Hassan

When I turned 12 years old, there were a lot of problems in my family. My sister was placed in a group home and when she returned home, we started to compete for attention. We both wanted all the attention, so we always fought. There were also problems between me and my father. It came to the point where I couldn't be at home anymore. So one week before my 13th birthday, I was put in my first group home, a diagnostic center in Brooklyn, New York.

This was hard for me to deal with, but luckily I never got picked on or into any fights because I was the youngest. The other residents saw me as a younger sister, and they always had my back.

You could stay at the diagnostic center for only three months.

Then they found you a placement. I really liked the girls who lived with me. I didn't want to leave and was scared to go to a new place. So as my three months came closer, I decided to run away.

I was on the run for about two months before the system caught up with me when I tried to get back in school. I was sent to another group home in Brooklyn. There were 12 girls there, including me.

This group home was different. The staff was very strict. When you came inside the house, they took your shoes and locked them in the office so you wouldn't be able to run away. When they dropped you off at school, they took your coat and you wouldn't get it back until they picked you up. So I never got to go in the school yard after lunch (it was January).

The girls were also different. Most of them were prejudiced. I have no reason to deny my ethnicity (which is Arabic, British, and Welsh). I look like I'm Puerto Rican but when people ask me, I tell them what I am with no shame. That's when I noticed the hate. The residents put down white people all the time, even the staff. I couldn't take it after a while. I could only think of trying to escape.

One day when it was time to get our snack out of the office (they locked up snacks, too), I snuck out with my shoes and went upstairs. After I put them on, I ran full speed from the second floor straight out the door. The lady who was in charge of the group home lived right next door and saw me run out. The next thing I knew, staff and residents were chasing me. They caught me, threw some slaps and punches, and dragged me back into the house.

I was going crazy. I figured there was no way to escape. I didn't have anyone to live for. No family. No friends. Only myself, and I was not happy at all. So I started thinking of how to end it all.

There was no way to get a knife because they had them locked in the office. So I went into the bathroom and searched the cabinets for pills, but found nothing. As I was on the bathroom floor crying hysterically, wondering what I was going to do, I remembered the cleaning supplies. So I wrote a note explaining everything and made myself a cocktail.

It tasted so nasty, but at least I wouldn't have to deal with my problems anymore. My stomach was killing me. I was so dizzy that I blacked out every now and then. The staff was asking, "What's going on?" They didn't know until I gave them my note and fell to the floor.

The next thing I remember I was waking up in Kings County Hospital. They put monitors on me and made me throw up what was left in my system. It tasted worse than the cocktail. I was alive and once again alone. The staff who came with me to the hospital said he was going out to get me something to eat. I haven't seen him since.

I was feeling like crap and so upset that my plan didn't work. I had to stay in the medical hospital for a week. Then they brought me to the "E" building, the mental ward for adolescents. They had big keys to open all the doors. It made me feel like I was back at the detention center. All I did was cry and say, "I don't belong here." I was getting highly depressed.

After a couple of months, I was diagnosed with a multiple personality disorder. They had me on various drugs. Those medicines had me sleeping a lot, and my mouth was always dry. I couldn't read or even look at pictures. That's how blurry my eyes were. My speech was messed up. I was pale, and I walked without picking up my feet.

I really started to hate the mental ward. Especially the doctors. I felt they didn't care. So I held in my feelings and when they became too built up, I would bug out. Then the female staff would try to put me in "four points" (tie my arms and legs to the bed) but I would fight it, so they would call the male staff from the boys' side. I would fight them, too!

After a while they overpowered me, especially when they put

that needle in my butt. There was no fighting that.

At one point, after they gave me a new drug, I went into seizures. I was so scared. My eyes were going in the back of my head. My body was going backward. It felt like my spine was going to crack in half. I really thought I was going to die. I wanted to, but not in so much pain.

I didn't know what to do. I was going crazy—crazier than when I came in. I was in the mental ward longer than almost all the other girls. I wanted to kill myself even more, but in there it was impossible; they made sure of it. So I decided that I was just going to have to deal with it, so I could eventually get out of there.

All the girls used to bug out. We used to take the bed and ride up and down the hallways on it. When the night staff fell asleep, we'd make crank calls. We had talent shows. We made plans to escape, even though we knew it was impossible. At times it was OK in there, but every night I cried myself to sleep.

> *She let me decide if I felt like talking, writing, or even if I felt like being quiet.*

Then one day, they gave me a social worker named Ms. Mensing. At first I really wasn't into her because I didn't like anyone associated with the hospital. I felt they just wrote down everything to get a paycheck, but now I must say, "God bless Ms. Mensing," because she was beautiful inside and out.

She let me have more control over what I wanted to do. She let me decide if I felt like talking, writing, or even if I felt like being quiet. She never had a book in her hand, writing down every word I said.

At first I didn't talk much with her. I only said, "I don't belong here. I want to leave!" But because Ms. Mensing acted and talked to me with respect, her special way got me to open up.

irst I talked about everything I hated—the hospital, the staff, the girls, and the rules. Then gradually I talked more

and deeper. I really needed and wanted to talk. I felt deep in my heart that I finally found someone I could confide in. I felt she really did understand me.

Ms. Mensing never changed my words around. She showed she cared for my feelings. If she had to notify a higher authority about something, she would tell me, not like other staff who did it behind my back. I was finally able to express my feelings to her and shared poems that I had written. She advised me to write down what was bothering me.

One day I wrote Ms. Mensing a poem, explaining what my father had done to me at home. She was the first person I ever told this to, and it hurt, but it has helped me feel better about it today.

**She made me feel good, which made me be good.**

Ms. Mensing was always there for me. She didn't care if my therapy hour for the day was up. She would still listen to me. I always used to wait for her at the door with the big keyhole.

In the hospital, they had levels you had to reach in order to have privileges, like going to school and going to the game room. Ms. Mensing told me to make my goal reaching the next level, and when I reached that goal, she would reward me. She took me to the grocery store. She bought me books to read and writing materials. But most of all, she shared my happiness and always gave me a hug, a sincere hug, and said, "Congratulations, Samira, you did it. I knew you could."

One time she got permission to take me outside, and we had a little picnic. That day we talked friend to friend, not therapist to client. We talked about a boy I had a crush on. We talked about things we liked, and about how I wanted to become a lawyer and a writer. I even told her how I thought my caseworker looked like a killer clown. We just laughed.

When I finally reached the highest level, she took me to Kings Plaza Mall. We tried on funny hats and rode the carousel. I had a lot of fun. I know in my heart that she did, too.

Ms. Mensing knew my love for writing. I always shared my poems and stories with her. She bought me my first journal. She made me feel good, which made me be good. Finally, after seven months, she arranged my discharge to a beautiful house in an agency called Boys Town.

Since then, I've been in many other group homes and foster homes and have had many experiences to remember. But last year I turned 18 and got away from it all (discharged). In January I moved to Florida to live with my aunt so that I would have no distractions in getting my high school diploma. But I do look forward to coming back to New York to pursue my career and to hopefully reunite with Ms. Mensing.

I face depression often, but now it's different because I have a better way of dealing with it. I probably go through a notebook every two weeks but I am able to face my feelings and deal with them, thanks to Ms. Mensing.

If Ms. Mensing is reading this, I would like to say thank you so very much for all your time, warmth, and support. Without you, I never would have made it.

---

*Samira was in high school when she wrote this story.*

# Worried Sick

### By Megan Cohen

I think too much. Not just about really troubling things, but about everything. It takes me 10-15 minutes to figure what to order off a menu, for example. There've been times when I've been up late doing a project and I can't get to sleep because I'm so worried about how I'll feel when the alarm clock wakes me up. I always thought it was a little weird, but I didn't realize how bad my problem was until last year, in 10th grade.

That year, I had two good friends at school—one from 9th grade and a new girl who'd just transferred there in 10th. As I started to get close to the new girl, I became obsessively worried that she'd become closer with my other friend than she was with me, and then they'd exclude me. I was afraid I'd lose two of the people I cared most about.

Sure enough, they did start to bond, probably because they

were annoyed at my constant worrying about the issue. Soon they began to hang out without telling me. Our school lunches became filled with awkward silences in which I felt completely isolated. These silences grew into crushing moments that another friend called "silences of death."

My paranoia didn't stop there. Since I was always thinking about them being such good friends, I began to devalue my other friendships. Sure, my other friendships were fun, but how deep were they? Had we ever cried together? Really delved into our histories? I began to create a mental checklist. Nobody passed.

> **I began to create a mental checklist for my friendships. Nobody passed.**

In the end I was left with the one thing I'd been most afraid of: losing two friends. That's when I realized that my over-thinking was dragging me down. I wanted to know what I could do about my problem. My editor suggested I talk to an expert, so I called Jayme Albin, a cognitive-behavioral therapist.

I found out that cognitive-behavioral therapy (CBT) is a type of counseling that focuses on how our thinking influences how we feel and what we do. We all have immediate thoughts when we react to a situation, and these thoughts are based on how we see the world—our "core belief system." The way we see things is based mainly on genetics and our past experiences, including how we were raised.

For example, let's say you get a 75 on a test. A reasonable reaction might be, "I didn't study hard enough for this test, but if I study harder for the next one I'll do better." But if you've grown up believing that, "If things aren't 100% perfect, I'm a failure," your immediate thought when you look at your grade might be, "I'm an idiot and I'll never get into college." That can cause anxiety.

Albin explained that my over-thinking is actually a form of anxiety. Anxiety can be useful in small amounts. "It helps us focus, study harder, and so on. It does serve a purpose," Albin said. "It becomes a problem when it starts interfering with everyday life."

But you can't magically get rid of the core beliefs that cause anxiety. "You can't just say, 'Don't be anxious.' That's not helpful," said Albin. It's hard to change your core belief system because it's so deeply ingrained in you, but you can change the way you think.

That's where CBT comes in, according to Albin. "Cognitive behavioral therapy challenges the automatic thoughts in a given situation," she said. The therapist helps you rethink the situation so that you have a more reasonable reaction to it.

> **Now I can tell when I'm about to obsess over a situation, and I'm starting to understand why I do it.**

So when you're feeling anxious, you can learn to think your way out of it by telling yourself that the thoughts causing your anxiety are irrational. Then you try to rethink the situation in a more rational way, until eventually that way of thinking just starts coming naturally.

CBT usually lasts about 12-18 weeks. By the time you leave therapy you should be so used to thinking yourself through tricky situations that you can sort of act as your own therapist. So, though I'd only met with Albin once and not for the usual 12 weeks, I decided to try just that.

Albin suggested I start by keeping a thought diary for a few weeks. I was supposed to write down every time I was overthinking or feeling anxious. Then I had to identify and write down the immediate thought that had made me feel that way. If I was feeling worried about my friends being close, maybe my initial thought had been, "They're going to exclude me today." I also had to come up with alternative thoughts to the irrational ones I usually have when I over-think.

If I were in therapy, my therapist and I would then sit down and look at my behavioral pattern. "We'd look to uncover what your tendencies are, like being a perfectionist," said Albin.

Once we saw how I reacted in certain situations, we would talk about how I could've reacted differently. I'd be able to start changing my thoughts and, eventually, my behavior.

For three weeks I wrote in the diary every time I found myself thinking about something too long. In my first entry I wrote, "Today I couldn't even decide what I wanted for lunch, let alone who to eat it with. An everything bagel with butter or a plain bagel with tuna? Or maybe pizza?"

I was frustrated with my indecisiveness, but I didn't use the reasoning process Albin had suggested. It seemed stupid for something as small as picking out lunch. I figured it would take more energy to chart out my thoughts than to just make a decision.

But writing down my thoughts over the three weeks made me realize how often I can't make the most trivial decisions, like whether to turn right or left on a street corner. I started to realize how much energy indecision takes from me. I also started to realize why I over-think sometimes.

One night about a week into my diary experiment, I "yelled" at a friend online, telling him he ignored me and thought he was superior to me. Even as I was accusing him, I didn't know why I was doing it.

I finally asked myself what I was doing, and realized that I was stressed and worried about another friend of mine. My anger had nothing to do with the person I'd yelled at. I told him to forget about everything I'd said, that I hadn't meant to take it out on him. I wrote in my diary that night, "This feels like a crucial point of progress and something I definitely would've overlooked before."

Now I can tell when I'm about to obsess over a situation, and I'm starting to understand why I do it. When I'm upset, I try to block out what's really upsetting me by upsetting myself over something less important.

## Analyze This!

And I'm still not sure why I over-think decisions like what I want to eat for lunch. Maybe I'm afraid of making the wrong choice and having nobody to blame for it but myself, even if it's just lunch. Now I realize that I just need to let it go and decide.

A couple of weeks ago, my notoriously anxious middle-aged cousin came to visit my family. It's hard to spend time with her because she's always worrying that things that are going just fine will fall apart, like she'll suddenly lose her job one day. She creates an unbearable uneasiness around her. She gave me a glimpse into what I could become if I don't stop this now.

I think I'm getting better already. At least I've decided one thing: I don't like that I over-think. It took me a really long time to figure that out, but I've finally gotten here. Now I just need to notice when I'm doing it, and then rethink the situation more rationally. This is one decision I'll be sure to stick to.

---

*Megan was 17 when she wrote this story.*
*She graduated high school and attended college.*

# Explaining Cognitive-Behavioral Therapy

### By La'Quesha Barner

When my editor told me about cognitive-behavioral therapy (CBT), I was surprised to hear that not all therapy is the same. I found out that CBT is a kind of a therapy that focuses on how you think and act, and how you can change. I thought that sounded useful. To learn more, we went to see Dr. Carrie King, a psychologist who works with kids and teens using CBT.

When I got to Dr. Carrie's office I was shocked at first, because it was not what I thought a therapist's place is supposed to look like. I thought all therapists had a long stretched out couch for the clients, in a not-so-comfortable room where you feel stuck.

But Dr. Carrie's office was a nice-sized room so you wouldn't feel trapped. She has a little playroom for the kids she sees, and inside her office are two comfy chairs, two big, wide windows,

53

a bookshelf and her own kitchen set-up with a microwave and a mini-refrigerator.

I'm new at interviewing and I was nervous, but Carrie was a very comfortable person to talk to. And the more she explained CBT, the more interested I became. I found out CBT is very different than what I thought therapy was supposed to be.

Carrie explained that "cognitive" means thinking, and behavior is how you act. So "cognitive-behavioral therapy" is therapy that looks at your thoughts and your actions and how they affect each other.

"What CBT therapists do is make people explain the thoughts that led up to their behavior," Carrie said.

"The biggest difference between CBT and regular therapy is that in CBT, the therapist asks you to do things," Carrie told me. "In other kinds of therapy, the therapist does less. They listen a lot, and they help you think about your life, but they don't tell you to do something. In CBT, you get homework: the therapist will ask you to try something out and then report back on how it went."

I thought that was cool, and that getting homework is probably good for patients who don't know what to do about their problems and need some direction. She gave me an example.

"If you were having a problem getting out of bed in the morning, I might ask you to keep a diary of all the times you didn't feel like getting out of bed, and what you were thinking during those times. And then you'd bring it in the next week and we'd talk about it."

Carrie says she uses CBT because she works with lots of teens and kids, and this kind of therapy works particularly well for us. "CBT involves a lot of practicing and role-playing," Carrie told me. "That's much easier for kids than just talking about their feelings." Carrie and her patients act out the kinds of situations that the kids have problems with, so they can see why they react the way they do and practice responding differently.

Carrie said that another difference between CBT and other therapy is that CBT focuses on the present, not the past. I always figured that in therapy they make you go back to the past to find out why you act the way you do. But Carrie said that in CBT, they only talk about the past if you want to. That was kind of confusing to me. How can you get to the core of the problem if you don't know how it started?

Carrie explained that CBT therapists believe you can accomplish more if you work on the behaviors, thoughts, and feelings that are most accessible—the ones that are occurring right now. "You can't touch the past or change it, so you should focus on what the past is doing to you right now, and change what is happening for you at this moment," she said. "CBT does care about the root of a problem, and the therapist will search for that root. But most of the therapy is focused on trying to change what you don't like about what's happening now. We have a clear goal, and we work until we reach it."

**CBT focuses on the present, not the past.**

I liked the sound of that. Picking a goal to work on seems more effective to me than just talking about whatever comes to mind. I wondered how you would find a therapist who works with CBT.

"You'd have to ask," Carrie told me. "You'd have to say, 'I'd like to see a therapist who uses CBT.' And with any kind of therapy, you have to go and meet the person and see if you like them."

"You'd also want to ask the therapist's opinion about whether CBT would be useful for you. I'd go and say, 'This is my problem, this is my goal, do you think CBT would work?' If the therapist is good, they'll be honest with you about whether they can help you or not."

"Sometimes, people need help figuring out what their problem is—they feel bad, but they don't know why—and CBT is not a great place for them. But if it's something like, 'I'm afraid to leave my house'—well, that's a very narrow, clear problem, and CBT can help."

I'd always been a little afraid of therapists, and I thought therapy was for crazy people. But I would certainly go to a CBT therapist. It seems like they just get to the point. I thought therapy meant you lay back on a couch and talk while the therapist does something else, and then you get medicated. But in CBT, they make you focus on what's really getting in the way of your life, so that you can face forward to the future.

> **"We have a clear goal, and we work until we reach it."**

---

*La'Quesha was 16 when she wrote this story.*

# A Shy Girl Finds Her Voice

### By Mayra Sierra

Growing up in Colombia, I used to be *fresca*. I would say whatever was in my head. I would tell you straight out how I felt about you. But then I came to New York when I was 13, and it was a different world.

In Colombia, I lived with family and I felt comfortable acting however I wanted. In New York, though, I lived with strangers and had to learn a new language and different manners. I came into foster care soon after I got here, and I guess that was too much for me because I wasn't *fresca* any longer. Instead I became a shy, shy girl.

About three years ago my social worker came up to me and told me to go to therapy—just like that! I thought, "But I'm not crazy! Why does she want me to go to therapy?" My social worker said I only had to check it out, and if I didn't like it I didn't have to stay. So like that I agreed.

She told me that the program was called Turtle Bay Music School and was open every Friday. So the next Friday I went. I had to take the train, which I wasn't used to. Thank God I got there fine. I walked into the building, which looked like a school with a big green flag out front—fine. I went upstairs—fine—and spoke to a staff member who told me to go to the waiting area. That wasn't fine. I didn't want to wait in that room, because some other kids were in there and I felt really shy.

> **Playing the instruments makes me feel relaxed. I release the anger that I carry inside.**

At the time, I had this problem that when I heard someone laughing, I'd think, "They must be laughing at me." When I heard someone talking, I'd think, "They must be talking about me." So for me to go to a room full of kids talking and laughing was like a mission impossible.

I told the lady that I just couldn't do it. I almost started crying—that's how scared I was! The lady was nice enough to notice that I wasn't kidding, so she let me wait by myself.

So far, I wasn't liking the program too much. Then Diane talked to me. Diane had an open, friendly face. She told me that she would be my therapist and she would also be in charge of the group I would be in. I liked her. She seemed really nice, sweet and caring. She also noticed that I was scared and just spoke to me calmly, which gave me comfort.

I thought therapy would be like in the movies, where the crazy person lays on a long couch while the therapist sits on a straight chair listening and taking notes. Instead we went to a big room with three tall windows, a desk, a piano, and a dark red carpet. For about half an hour, Diane and I sat talked about school, friends, life, things I like and things I don't like. I thought it went pretty smoothly.

After that, I had group. I was nervous, but it was a group of 13- and 14-year-old girls, which was good. We played instruments and made music or listened to each other talk.

We had drums, a piano, maracas, guitars, and tambourines. I felt kind of stupid making noise with those instruments. I wondered, "What the hell am I doing?" Because if you think about it, sitting in a circle with girls and just making noise with an instrument—isn't that kind of stupid?

It took me a while to understand that I could express how I was feeling through music. I could make any sound that I liked to express how angry, calm, excited, or sad I was, just by making the sound louder, lower, slower, or faster. I learned that I like playing the drums, especially. When I am mad, I can hit them very hard and make a BOOM!

Expressing my emotions through music does help. It's better to beat a drum than hit someone and get into trouble. I tend to keep all my feelings inside and I know that's not good, because sooner or later I will explode. Playing the instruments makes me feel relaxed. I release the anger that I carry inside.

After my first day, I felt comfortable with the people there. I decided to go back every Friday. The program is only for foster care kids, so I knew the other girls had gone through some of the things that I have. It felt nice to know that I wasn't the only girl in the world who's had problems with her family.

Before I went to Turtle Bay, I usually didn't talk to anyone about my feelings. I thought people might not understand me and I didn't want to bother them with my problems. I also worried that people would pity me or make me feel embarrassed about asking for their help.

Last year, I was going through a rough period and I had a school project due that I couldn't finish, so I talked to the teacher (who was really nice) and explained what I was going through to see if he could give me another day. My friend overheard and said, "Oh, Mayra, you are just using your problems as an excuse." I couldn't believe what she said. It made me feel like I should keep my feelings to myself.

But talking to my therapist is not like talking to friends or family. I know Diane won't tell anyone because it's her job to keep everything confidential. And when we talk about how I feel, she really listens. It makes me feel more confident to know that she's listening and not laughing at what I say.

Over the last three years, Diane has helped me understand myself and realize that there's nothing wrong with expressing my feelings and saying what I think. We talk over a problem and she asks me questions about what I'm really trying to say and how I want to solve it.

Since I started working with Diane, I have done many things that I don't think I could've done three years ago, because I would've been too scared. The biggest thing is that I spoke up to my mother. I was always scared of her because she was abusive. She used to hit us a lot, so I used to do everything that she wanted. Even now that she lives in Colombia and I live here, I've always been afraid to tell her no.

But recently I had a big fight with my mother because my brother told her that I liked a guy and my mother got mad. She was screaming like crazy and calling me names. So I screamed back at her, saying, "If I'm a slut, I learned that from you." She started crying and hung up on me.

After that I didn't speak to my mother for more than two weeks. Those two weeks were hard because I usually talk to her almost every day. But after I had that big argument with her our relationship changed. I started to say no to her more often, and I tell her what I think about her actions, which I never did before. I feel closer to her now and I don't feel so scared of her anymore.

Turtle Bay is more than just therapy, though. It's a place that helps teens like me feel comfortable. Turtle Bay always has dinner for us to eat after group sessions and gifts on holidays. The therapists take us out to the movies, to eat, and to go bowling. We also put on a show where kids perform songs or poems for friends and family.

For me and the other members of the program, Turtle Bay is like a big family. In three years I've learned a lot—to understand my circumstances and not to let them get to me, to be strong and keep on going, to open up. Everyone learns something different, because each one of us has a different problem. But we all have one thing in common. We have a program that helps us deal with our fears.

---

*Mayra was 17 when she wrote this story. She later earned her GED and got a job at her former foster care agency.*

# Listening to My Inner Child

### By Aquellah Mahdi

The idea that I had an "inner child" came from my therapist at Renfrew, a treatment center where I went to get help for my eating disorder and the years of abuse I'd suffered as a child. My therapist mentioned quite a few times that my "inner child" needed comfort and protection. I really didn't understand what she meant by that.

She said my inner child was the little voice that goes, "tell them what's bothering you." She said that I try to stuff her down in the bottom of my life and never allow her to speak, and that I needed to let her speak and listen to what she had to say.

So I started with letters. The letters were from my inner child at different ages. My 7-year-old self wrote her own story about the things that she remembered at that age, and I couldn't believe it. The assignment was helpful because at each age my inner child taught me something different about how I survived. This helped me remember that as a young child I had the willpower and courage to get through all the abuse.

Then one day in art therapy I was told to make a containment box and put whatever I wanted inside of it, anything that has caused me any kind of pain, or just whatever was on my mind. While I was looking through a box of different fabrics I came across a cloth doll. I think I chose the doll because she seemed to be in the wrong place. She was different, just like me. She came to represent my inner child.

I placed her in my box. I wrapped her in red cloth and string and said, "This is her casket." I figured I put her into the containment box to hold her in a place where no one could get in. So no one could ask her questions and find out what made her feel that she was unsafe, uncharted, or desolate. Outside of the containment box I drew colors intertwined to keep whatever was inside the box trapped in there so it would never be able to come out. I needed to put all of my problems into the box.

When I picked her up from the box her blank face and delicate body reminded me of how delicate and lost I feel. How I

**The words started to slowly flow, like a river that is partially paused by a huge tree limb.**

want to just hide. So on my doll's cloth body I drew a compass. For each direction there was a different word.

Her stomach was commingled with the guilt, shame, and pain of the inner secrets. On her face there were no words, just a blank area. No eyes, mouth or nose. On her right arm there was the word pain, on her left there was the word confused. On her legs were the words lost and shame.

When it was time to take her out of the box I did so but I left the cloak draped around her arms to keep the scars covered, so I didn't have to talk to anyone about what each word represented. That was something my inner child and I decided would remain hidden. But it would be written on her body, so that one day we would each tell our own story. The story of how the abuse had affected us, and our own recovery process.

Then a day came when I couldn't take it anymore. She was suffocating me. She had something to say and I had promised I would allow her to speak her mind when she felt ready.

That day in a private session of art therapy I actually let her out of the box and took off her cloth, to expose the naked words I had written on her body. I held her in my hands to face her. I was in some kind of trance. It was time for her to let go of the demons and time for me to listen, to understand what the child inside of me felt like. She felt trapped, stuck in a world of broken innocence and confusion.

**I was angry that I had worked a lot and I had no place where I could go to keep on working.**

I needed to assure her that everything was now safe. I felt like I wasn't ready. The art therapist asked about the first word, what it meant. I opened my mouth to speak, but all I was doing was mouthing what my inner child wanted to say.

I wanted to keep her silenced. I felt like she was actually going through the things she wanted to say. Her body was back in the bitter cold night of her father's ruling; she couldn't escape. I had to help her break her body away from that past trauma.

I watched the clock. Then the words came. Not as easily as I'd thought. But they started to slowly flow, like a river that is partially paused by a huge tree limb. I sat and listened to her speak. My inner child was talking, and what a lovely but frightening sound it was.

I don't want to repeat what she said, but afterwards I had the feeling of inner peace. I still felt a bit unsure about what I had just heard—her side of the story, the vivid memories in my mind. I thought, "How could she remember all of the terror?" But I knew that it was a step in the right direction.

This was the first time I had ever listened to my inner self. It was the only time I didn't try to stuff her under a pillow and say, "be quiet," or, "your feelings will go away." It was all her time. She cried, but they were tears of relief and patience. She'd been waiting for me to allow someone to come in, fondly greet us both, and give us a place where it could all start to come out.

Not long after that I left Renfrew. I was told my insurance wouldn't pay for me to stay there any longer.

My inner child doll lay on my bed on top of the things I would soon be placing in my suitcase. I picked her up and looked at her. "I don't need you anymore," I said. "I'm fine. Anyway, no one will have the time to sit and let either of us continue what we had to say." I believed that many people would think that after my stay at Renfrew my mind and soul should be healed. That I should be OK. But Renfrew was only the beginning.

"She has already been protected and comforted," I thought. "I have listened." I was angry at my inner child. I was angry that I had worked a lot and I had no place where I could go to keep on working. I walked out the door and she stayed. She was placed neatly in the red cloak, tied with string, on top of a pile of garbage.

As I walked away from her I felt like she was yelling to get my attention, for me to turn around. I knew I wouldn't get far without her. I believed that when I threw her away that day the process of either one of us continuing to recover was also thrown away.

For now, I have stuffed her back into that world. I keep her hushed with no plan to let her surface. But remembering when I let her come to the light that day, I wonder if I might ever do it again.

## Analyze This!

As I get closer to my adult years she needs to come out and speak much more often, just so that she is reminded of who she is and what she means to me. She is someone who was—and in a way still is—trapped in a past world of turmoil. But she holds the key to what can help me grow into a complete woman. If I do want to go forward, I have to go backwards. That step back means giving her the time to speak. Time for me to listen, and let her heal.

---

*Aquellah was 20 when she wrote this story.*
*She went to college to study nursing and art therapy.*

# Learning to Forgive My Mom

### By Christopher B.

Every time I would see my mother we would argue. She would bring up things that happened in the past and throw them in my face. I found it hard to forgive her for the problems we had in the past that led me to end up in a detention center. My social worker, Ms. Davis, knew my relationship with my mother was not good and urged me to go to therapy. Ms. Davis wanted to see us get along better.

I didn't want to go to any stupid therapy to talk about the problems I had with my mother. I felt I would be wasting my time, because my relationship with her wasn't going to get better.

Ms. Davis told me I had to go therapy because it was part of my "service plan" while I was in the system. I felt like I was being forced to do something I didn't want to do. But I finally

## Analyze This!

decided to go because I didn't want to end up going to another group home.

I started going to therapy on Saturdays. Ms. Smith was the name of my therapist. I could see that she had a nice personality from the way she spoke to the kids and their mothers. We spoke briefly in her office for the first time. She was very patient and I felt comfortable talking to her. She explained that she wasn't going to try to rush me into expressing myself about my problems with my mother. She wanted me to get to know her better before I started confiding in her.

I didn't like talking about my problems with anybody. I felt like I couldn't trust anybody. I had been hurt a lot by many loved ones who were supposed to be in my corner when times got rough. They let me down big time by misusing the trust I had in them.

By going to therapy each week, I started to express myself better. I took my time telling Ms. Smith about my problems to see if I could trust her. I told her it was going to be difficult forgiving my mother because I was still carrying so much anger.

My mother always tried to call me at the group home. I would tell the staff that I didn't want to speak to her. She would leave messages for me to call her. I didn't want to have anything to do with her. I had been making it without her, so why did I need her now? When I saw her on the streets, I would walk past her without saying anything.

The reason why things got this bad between us was because my mother treated me the same way my father treated her. My father mentally abused my mother. He would always try to belittle her every time they argued. I always felt my mother acted out her anger towards me because my father treated her badly. I always found it harder to get along with her than my sisters did. She always treated me differently from them. She went shopping with them and spent time with them. I reacted by spending a lot of time away from home to avoid her.

## Learning to Forgive My Mom

When I went to therapy one Saturday, Ms. Smith wanted me to talk about what happened to cause me to end up in a detention center. I told Ms. Smith that one night my mother and I got in a huge fight when I came home very late and disrespected her by talking back to her. I told her that my mother got really upset and that she tried to hit me with a chair. When I blocked it with my hands, the chair fell back on top of her. She then tried to hit me on the head with a glass vase. My sister's boyfriend got in front of me and blocked her swing with his hands. My mother cut his hands so badly that he had to go to the hospital and get stitches.

I started getting upset while I was telling my therapist what happened to me. She stopped me for a minute so I could calm myself down. I was very emotional and frustrated while talking about my problems.

When we continued, I told Ms. Smith how my mother came to court and accused me of cutting my sister's boyfriend with a piece of glass. She also told the court how I hit her with a chair and how she had to go to the doctor. I was locked up in a detention center for two weeks before going to jail for one and a half years. I felt one and a half years were taken away from me for no reason.

*I took my time telling Ms. Smith about my problems to see if I could trust her.*

Ms. Smith told me that I had to learn how to forgive and release the pain inside me. She said the first step in forgiving someone is to really mean it from the heart. I heard what she said but I didn't know if I was ready to make that first step. I didn't know if I was ready to open up my heart to my mother and forgive her.

I left therapy that day feeling like a better person. I finally got the chance to release some anger by talking about my problems. During my ride on the train I was thinking about my mother and what Ms. Smith said about forgiving. I knew everybody makes mistakes and they deserve a second chance.

# Analyze This!

Mother called me around 7 o'clock that same night. Lisa, one of the staff workers, asked me if I wanted to speak to her. I took the phone and I told her that we needed to talk things out. My mother agreed and she sounded very good. She wanted me to come to the house after school.

I went to see my mother the next day. I wanted to talk to her about the problems that we had. I realized as I got older that I was at fault for some of the problems because I never listened to anybody and I wanted things to be done my way. I had to stop feeling sorry for myself because I ended up in a detention center. I wanted to tell her how sorry I was that I didn't listen to her, and that I disrespected her by coming home any time I felt like when I was living with her. I wanted to tell her how I felt about her as a mother, and how I wanted to start a new relationship as mother and son.

She was cooking dinner for my two sisters when I walked in the kitchen. My mother asked me how I was doing in school and in my group home. I was nervous to be under the same roof with her, because this was the first time in two years that I was able to come home to visit. I didn't want the same thing to happen as when the cops had to remove me from my house. I went into my big sister's room to talk with her until my mother was finished cooking dinner.

My mother called me from my sister's room to have dinner and talk with her alone at the table. She told me how sorry she was for coming to court and seeing me end up in jail. She said she was hurt by the way I was treating her that night. I told my mother that I forgave her and I wanted to start a new relationship with her and just move on.

I could see tears running down her cheeks when she told me I was the only son that God gave her and she loved me tremendously. I stood up to hug my mother because I knew she really meant every word she said.

My relationship with my mother is much better than it has been in the past. We are able to communicate better and get along well. I can go to the house any time I want and eat. I can go home on weekend passes and I spend all the major holidays with her.

The reason why our relationship has changed is because we both realize that everybody makes mistakes and deserves a second chance. I had to realize that I couldn't just blame my mother for what she did. If I had listened to her when she told me to come in the house early, she would have never been put in a situation of being worried and angry about my disobedience.

I'm glad my relationship with my mother has gotten much better, but we still have problems. I'm able to deal with them better and talk about them without holding any negative feelings inside. If it wasn't for therapy, my relationship with my mother would still be the same. I just wanted her to love me the same way she loved my two sisters.

**My mother and I started going to therapy together to try to prevent what happened in the past from ever happening again.**

My mother and I started going to therapy together to try to prevent what happened in the past from ever happening again. It was hard being in therapy with her because I was afraid that she was going to get mad if I said something she didn't like. My mother is the type of person who gets offended easily and is not afraid to defend herself. When I was in therapy alone it was easier to express myself and the room was less tense, but eventually I got used to being in therapy with her. We spoke about the problems we had in the past. I felt wonderful on the inside because we were able to communicate and be in the same room together.

I feel our relationship is better, but I wouldn't want to destroy it by rushing home before I'm ready. I want to take it slow in developing a good relationship with my mother. But if some-

# Analyze This!

thing terrible happened to her health and she needed me at home to take care of her, I wouldn't even think twice about packing my bags and going to be by her side. I love her with all my heart, even though we had a lot of problems in the past.

---

*Christopher was 18 when he wrote this story. He graduated from college with a degree in political science and sociology, and then attended graduate school.*

# Family Therapy: A Safe Place to Connect

*Adrienne Williams-Myers, a licensed clinical social worker, explains how therapy can support families who are reunifying after foster care:*

**Q: How can therapy help families reconnect?**

**A:** When parents and kids are involved in the system, their world has been full of other people telling them what to do. Therapy is a time for them to focus on themselves and their goals. I help families identify their strengths and love for each other, and to really work on building on those so they can stay together.

By learning how they overcame the troubles that led to their separation, families can use their strengths to get through the confusing emotions and tensions that come with reunification.

**Q: What do parents and kids often feel when they've been separated?**

# Analyze This!

**A:** The parent usually comes in feeling a tremendous amount of guilt because she didn't do what she needed to do to prevent children from being removed. Mothers may also blame the system or the school system for making the call, or blame the other parent or relatives that didn't support her.

Sometimes mothers still feel angry that the way they punished their children was considered abuse. Many times they will tell us, "My mom hit me, my teachers hit me. What's the problem? I'm fine."

> *Therapy can help make a safe place for everyone in the family to express themselves.*

For the children, there's a lot of anger and anxiety about ending up back in care again. The little ones, especially, feel a lot of separation anxiety. They're anxious and fearful that the system will take them away again, and they've lost trust in their parents' ability to protect them.

Older children tend to be angry and to blame the parent. They need a period of time to get to know the parent again and to feel comfortable trusting the parent. If substance abuse issues led to the child going into foster care, they need to be sure that mom is not picking up again.

**Q: What are some techniques that help parents and kids get to know each other?**

**A:** In family therapy, I help them get to know and trust each other, mostly by allowing them simply to talk and hear each other. Sometimes I ask them to write feelings or experiences down in journals, or to talk into a tape recorder and then listen to themselves. I ask them to watch each other communicate, including all forms of communication: words, body language, hugging and kissing.

I'll ask them things like, "How do you see yourself positively? How do you think mom or teacher sees you positively? Or how do you think your child sees you positively? Tell me six great things about yourself." I'll ask them to write it down and share it with each other. Sometimes they're kind of shocked to find out that mom sees them in a positive light, or that the other people in their family notice the same positive things.

At some point, I'll also ask the kids to say what they went through in foster care to help their parents understand that painful time. If it's too upsetting, they can write it down and hold it for a while before sharing it, or even mail it.

Therapy can help make a safe place for everyone in the family to express themselves, especially to express the anger in a healthy way. It's better if children and parents don't hold that anger inside or express it in blowups.

Therapy can also help moms work on the behaviors that will help their children trust them again. A parent who was using drugs or drinking usually was in the habit of making false promises and not following through. Moms can learn how to be there for their kids by making only the promises they can follow through on. Becoming a trusting family again really happens one day at a time.

# Searching for Dr. Right

### By Maya Noy

I have been in and out of therapy for as long as I can remember. So far, it has felt like a complete waste of time. But even though I've had a lot of bad experiences with therapists, I'm still looking for one who can help me.

Right now, I have a job and have been living on my own since I left foster care six years ago, but I feel so anxious and depressed every day. I don't know if therapy is the answer, but I feel alone in the world and I want some guidance.

It's no fun looking up therapists, calling around, visiting different clinics, and repeating my sad, pathetic story over and over again. Especially since one reason I need therapy is to get help with my anxiety, which makes it extremely difficult to deal with strangers. Then there's the depression, which for me means not having the desire to get up and face the day.

I get nervous even before I pick up the phone. My heart beats fast and my tummy feels funny. When they ask why I want to come for therapy, I want to say, "Because I'm a nutcase, duh!" Instead I usually say, "I have general anxiety—about life and my relationships." Sometimes I talk about "my friend," because pretending to be someone else makes it easier.

When I get to the office for the intake—the first meeting—I tell them I have been in talk therapy for years, and that I feel I need a more direct approach than I've gotten. They usually nod and agree and we set up another appointment.

Then it's all downhill. At the next appointment, I am so eager to finally be able to talk to a willing party that I rarely remember that I actually need advice! And they let me go on and on. I leave making excuses, like, "That was only our first (or second, or third) meeting. We need time to work on my issues. And they have to hear my issues before they can help." That pattern goes on for weeks, maybe months.

Then I usually quit therapy because I don't feel the person is "getting" me. I am never sure how to speak up and tell the person that I'm not happy with the therapy. There have been rare occasions when I try to explain, but I don't like to hurt anyone's feelings, so I usually wimp out and run instead. I don't think I've ever been in therapy more than a few months at a time.

I thought that in therapy I would talk about my childhood and the therapist would help me discover why I am anxious and depressed now, and talk with me about how to break the thought patterns that are keeping me down. Most of the problems I deal with now are directly related to feeling unwanted as a child. In my mind, if my own mother didn't want me, then I am worthless, and everything I do is worthless. I don't know how to get past that.

I want to work on letting some of the past go. It's a huge burden to carry around each day. But when therapists ask only, "How are you?" or, "How was your week?" I feel limited to only talking about the present. And that hasn't helped me so far.

# Analyze This!

One therapist was a young lady who appeared younger than I was (27) and had a happy-go-lucky personality, almost too happy. She would start by saying, "How are you?" and end by saying, "See you next week," with little else in between.

Oh, and once she wrote me a prescription. It read:

#1 Look in mirror every morning and say to self, "I am pretty."

#2 Take one bath for at least 20 minutes once a week.

How could either of those "medicines" help me with my childhood pain, or my adult anxiety and strained relationships? Was I missing something? With this therapist, I rambled and smiled nervously. There were long silences that I felt I had to fill. It was very nerve-wracking. So I ran.

Actually, first I called her supervisor and asked if I could see someone else because I wasn't comfortable with her. The supervisor told me that I should talk to her myself and explain that I was uncomfortable. "That would be good therapy for both of you," her supervisor said. That's when I ran.

> **I want to work on letting some of the past go. It's a huge burden to carry around each day.**

All I could imagine was saying the kinds of things that run through my mind, like, "Hey, you suck as a therapist. I'm outta here!" I didn't want to make her feel bad (wanting too much to be liked is a problem I have). And getting the proper words together is difficult, so I just avoid.

Looking back, I'm sure I could have brought it up gently, saying something like, "I have problems with confrontation, but I don't feel too comfortable…" But I want a therapist who would notice my discomfort, or notice something, and ask about that without me having to bring it up first.

Recently, I pondered my experiences. I asked myself, "Am I closing myself off from being helped?

But I wondered if anyone could be helped by the methods

of those therapists. Is it really therapeutic to let big long silences happen? Those silences just made me uncomfortable. I would feel it was up to me to fill them, and I would start rambling more and more. When I didn't get any response to what I said, I would just get anxious.

At most, some therapists have made sympathetic comments here and there, but I believe I need more than that. Ideally, I would like someone to actually engage in a conversation. I wonder if I am even on the right track in seeking therapy. Maybe I need a different kind of help. Maybe I need a life coach? Boot camp? Maybe therapy won't work for me because I often can't verbally express myself in a way that helps people understand how I feel.

Often I think back to the one good therapist I did have, Janet. This was a woman with a plan. Janet knew what she wanted to see happen during our sessions, and invited me to try things her way as opposed to just going with the flow. What most impressed me was that she actually asked questions and even took notes. I hadn't seen that in real life, just on TV. It showed me that she was interested in actually remembering our conversations, and would have something to refer back to if needed.

Janet told me that we should start with the past and work our way into the present, and maybe even the future. She started by talking about my childhood, and asked very specific questions about my life, how I grew up and what took place when. She even asked about my parents' backgrounds, and how my brother was raised so differently from me.

Often Janet would tell me little sayings that related to our conversations, or gave me exercises when I had issues that needed work. She even gave me options, such as, "We could work on the past for the entire session, unless there are important matters to discuss immediately, or we could dedicate the first half to the past, and the second half to the present." Janet seemed like a real person, not just a timer waiting to go off. I got the feeling that she was actually interested in helping me.

Best of all, she gave me resources when I had practical problems. If I said I couldn't afford diapers one week, she would tell me where to go. Or if I was considering taking a class or needed help finding a job, she would give me leads, like the name and number of a place where I could get help with those practical things.

I liked having a hands-on counselor, someone who would pick up the phone and make a call and tell me, "It's all taken care of, you just need to do this or that." It felt good to have a helping hand in addition to therapy. But just when I felt like we were getting somewhere, I had insurance problems and was not able to see her anymore. How's that for luck!

> **Finding a therapist is just like dating—sometimes you have to go on many dates before you meet The One.**

Now I'm looking for a therapist like her. Maybe I will meet Mr. or Ms. Right Therapist. It's just like dating—sometimes you have to go on many dates before you meet The One. (I don't enjoy first dates, either!)

Just recently I started seeing someone new. This therapist is nice and all, but I'm not totally confident in her abilities. She is a student, and I almost feel like a guinea pig. I am trying to be a little pushier about getting what I need, though.

Once I reminded the therapist that I was looking for feedback and asked, "Where is it?" She nodded and smiled, but I was in the middle of rushing through so many other things, just to get them off my chest, that I suppose we both dropped the subject.

At times I have asked her, "Am I rambling?" Her response to most things I ask is a blank stare and a smile. When she does comment, it is often polite, as if it's right out of a book, like: "You are working very hard in therapy, and you have accomplished things, which is a big step," etc.

## Searching for Dr. Right

Once again I'm feeling frustrated. But I am trying to care less about the therapist's response. Instead, I have learned that I have to work on myself. I listen to myself while I talk to her, and go from there.

Listening to my own words, I think it's obvious how my depression and anxiety are connected to my past. Growing up in an unhappy home, I didn't learn how to enjoy life, how to grow and live, instead of just exist. And I haven't been able to teach myself, because my fears get in the way. That's why I've been looking for a therapist who can show me steps to take to separate the old me, a miserable child, from the new me, a capable adult.

From listening to myself in therapy, I know that I am so stuck in the past. I am trying to get unstuck. But I am not sure it's helping me to try to be my own therapist. And hey, where's my check?

---

*Maya wrote this story as an alumni writer for Represent.*

# Therapy Changed My Life

**By Anonymous**

Therapy helped me let out a lot of anger I had locked inside. It changed my life, and it could change your life. It helped me to better myself.

My father used to beat me a lot for no reason at all (he was drunk about 99.9% of the time). He used to make me and my older brother Kevin go to the store and buy him beer and condoms. He sent us for condoms because he had several females coming to the house (not all at once). My father didn't care what time of day it was, he would make us run errands for him. I was only a young kid when I was being sent on errands.

As I got older, things got worse. One day my father went out and left me with one of his co-workers named Tracy. I never knew why my father did this. Tracy and I were in the living room watching TV and Tracy asked me if anybody was in the back room. I said no. I didn't think anything else about it. Tracy went in the back room and called me. I went in the back room. Tracy was sitting on one of the beds. Tracy called me over, so I went.

Next thing I knew, Tracy unzipped my pants and pulled them down. I was only 8 and I was very afraid. Then Tracy pulled down my underwear. Tracy told me to lay down on the bed, so I did. Tracy did the same thing I was told to do. Then Tracy lay down on the bed and forced me to have oral sex. This was my first sexual experience.

Later that night when it was all over, my brother Kevin came home and I told him what happened. My brother took me to a friend of my father's named Macho because he didn't know where my father was and he trusted Macho. Macho, who lived right around the corner, at first had mixed feelings when he heard what happened. He had known Tracy for so long that he couldn't believe Tracy would do such a thing. On the other hand, Macho trusted me and knew that I wouldn't lie to him.

I didn't know it, but Tracy had followed Kevin and me to Macho's house. When Tracy came in, Macho took his cane and started hitting Tracy until Tracy was just about unconscious. Then Macho's wife called the cops. The next thing I knew I was in the police station with my father and brother. I remember telling lots of cops and a therapist what happened. I remember having to demonstrate in front of some people with two dolls.

**I was a little shaky about telling perfect strangers my problems.**

I also remember the expression on my father's face when Ron and I were alone. It looked like he was upset, but not because of what Tracy did. Instead, it looked like he was mad at me for making him go through all this trouble. It was like I could read my father's mind, which said, "Damn! Why did you have to put me through all this bull?"

# Analyze This!

I went back home. I don't know if charges were ever pressed against Tracy. There was one good thing that came out of my ordeal—I never saw Tracy again. This experience was traumatic because Tracy was so much older than me and really unattractive, as I remember. Just imagine being forced to have oral sex, or any kind of sex with, let's say, your grandmother or grandfather—an experience I wouldn't wish on my worst enemy.

As I got older, my life with my father got worse. For a while he had stopped abusing me and Kevin, but after his girlfriend was killed in a car accident he started drinking, gambling, and abusing us mentally, physically, and verbally all over again. My Aunt Maroline decided to send me to my cousin's house when she found out what was going on.

But my cousin contributed to my problems by verbally and physically abusing me. I was thinking of running away, but I didn't know how.

One day when I was in the library I saw a book called "I Hate School." In the back of the book I saw the phone number for Covenant House. I called and made arrangements to go there the following day. The next day I put on three pairs of socks, two pair of pants, two shirts, and my flight jacket. In my book bag I had clothes instead of books. My cousin had no idea what I was doing because I packed my bag behind her back. When I stepped out the door I was very happy, because I felt I was leaving hell and going to heaven.

When I went to Covenant House, I was a little shaky about telling perfect strangers my problems, telling them things I had never told anyone else before.

While I was there I had to see a therapist. It was mandatory. I was in the waiting area for quite a while. Then I heard my name called. The therapist's name was Dr. Smith. I told Dr. Smith how my father abused me, and how I ended up living with my abusive cousin. And when I spoke about how I was abused sexually, mentally, verbally, and spiritually, I cried, and Dr. Smith did, too. That's when I realized that she was there to help me and not to hurt me.

Dr. Smith gained my trust in many different ways. One way she gained my trust was when my caseworker was going to send me back to my cousin's house. Dr. Smith fought to keep me from going back because she believed I was telling the truth. Another way she gained my trust was when I got dumped by a girl I really cared about and was on the brink of suicide. I was standing on the sidewalk crying. Dr. Smith was going to her car, about to go home, when she saw me shivering. She came over and asked me what was wrong and I said nothing. She knew something was wrong, so she walked me to her office. After about 10 minutes of silence I finally told her. The conversation wasn't over until an hour and a half later.

> **When I spoke about being abused I cried, and Dr. Smith did, too. That's when I realized that she was there to help me.**

After that, I felt like I was floating on air. I trusted Dr. Smith more than ever because she worked overtime and without pay just to help me with my problem. If I went to my father with a problem like that, he'd probably laugh in my face and walk away. From then on I felt that it wasn't just a therapist-client kind of thing. I felt it was a friendship and that we had an understanding with one another.

I had so much anger locked in for so long it almost drove me crazy. Every time I told my story to other counselors at Covenant House, I would add a little more because I was feeling more and more comfortable talking to people about my situation.

After a month or so I was placed in a group home. It was much more peaceful because it was on beachfront property. Whenever I was upset and didn't feel like talking to anyone, I would go out on the beach, sit down on the sand, and let the roars of the ocean tides cause my anger to drift away.

I didn't feel comfortable around the group home therapist, who was male. I felt more comfortable talking to a female about my problems, because Dr. Smith was like the mother I never had.

The group home therapist seemed more aggressive and more in a rush than Dr. Smith. Somehow he had found out that I had been a pyromaniac (a person who sets fires) and all he did was ask me the same questions. ("Do you fantasize about fire? Do you dream about fire? Are there voices in your head telling you to start fires?") 20 times in one minute. That annoyed the hell out of me. When he asked me if I wanted to talk about anything else (he did all the talking), I said no and left. After that first session I didn't go back.

**Finding a therapist who is right for you isn't always easy, but if do you find one, don't let 'em go.**

Finding a therapist who is right for you isn't always easy, but if do you find one that is right for you, don't let 'em go. If Dr. Smith was the therapist for my group home, I'd still be going to therapy. I still keep in contact with her because she's my best friend. From sessions with Dr. Smith, I learned that you don't have to be crazy to see a psychiatrist.

Even after therapy, I sometimes feel guilty and depressed. I wonder if, by running away from my cousin's house, I hurt my aunt who had me moved there. (My aunt says she still loves me.)

As for my brother Kevin, he has always stood by me. He never wanted anything to happen to me. But Kevin doesn't want to deal with his anger. Once, I told Kevin about the abuse at my cousin's house. Kevin said, "Is she feeding you? Is she giving you clothes?" I said yes, but she wasn't doing enough positive things to cover up the negative things that she was doing to me. Kevin never really wanted to hear about the negative. I didn't know why. We're different that way. I feel it's always better to look at a problem directly.

For example, Kevin still loves my father, even after all the stuff he put him through. Kevin is trying to cover up his feelings, but I don't think he should. I think that's why Kevin catches a temper sometimes (much quicker than I do). You can't criticize Kevin about one thing, even if it's constructive. I think Kevin should go to therapy like I did, because even though he's 20 and I'm 16, I'm more mature because I know how to control my anger by expressing it. I don't pretend everything's all right.

I still have a temper that I occasionally let out, mostly to counselors, sometimes to residents. But I'm much better at dealing with it than I was before.

If you have problems, don't keep them locked in or they will affect your life more than you think. If you keep your anger locked in, you might end up abusing your kids. Then they will either continue the cycle of abuse or run away from home like I did.

---

*The author was 16 when he wrote this story.*
*He later became a researcher for travel books.*

# A Hard Pill to Swallow

**By Gloria Williams**

My story is simple. It's about therapy and how it can sometimes help people. It's also about how being put on medication when you're not communicating well with your therapist can lead to some twisted turns.

When I was 5, I had to go to therapy. It was in this cool little spot right next to huge white house. The office was kind of like a house itself, with a living room. The secretary played classical music and they had the coolest kids' books. Back then I liked books about Clifford (the big red dog). That dog rocked!

My therapist was cool. She would say, "Hey, what's happening?" and our little get-togethers would go as smooth as whipped cream. She had nice eyes and blonde hair (you can bet it was real), and I could tell her things without feeling like she would tell my business.

We would talk about Mommy and Daddy, who were not together. They became the main subject—that and Mommy's sickness. She would say, "What's up with school?" and, "How are you feeling?" You know, the questions your parents would ask but you'd never tell the truth. Then she would say, "Tell me more."

We would talk for two hours or so while I played with the doctor set and this huge doll house (it was off the hook). I went to her for five years. She was a big help with a little girl's problems. Having her to talk to was a big relief.

After five years of seeing her, I moved and that meant a change of therapist. I loved my foster home and neighborhood where I'd lived and it killed me to leave. My new home was small, a shack compared to my old house. Plus, my foster mother was fake and had a 5-year-old son straight out of hell. I missed my old foster sister and brothers. I missed my therapist a whole lot, too.

I tried to push out the fact that this was my new home. I just stayed with my brother and chilled with him, but everything felt like it was from another planet.

I went to a new therapist, and she was not as good as I thought she would be. In fact, everything was worse than it had been at my old therapist's. The office had little paintings of children in fields on the walls, and the outside of the building was this dark brown stone (dull and nasty). I did not like going there.

I didn't want to start over with a new therapist, but part of me thought I should give her a chance. When I tried, though, I just couldn't connect. When I told my therapist something, she would almost always reply, "OK," in this tone that made me think she was really thinking, "Should I care?" Or she'd just nod, and in my mind I'd be like, "Hmmmm," or, "Whatever." She always seemed distant and uptight, not laid back and chill like my old therapist.

Then, every few weeks, she would not be there and I'd have to talk to some old geezer. He would just stare at me, then ask

## Analyze This!

another question. He made me uncomfortable, but he still expected me to share my world with him (please).

Sometimes I would talk, but other times I wouldn't say a thing. I knew I was wasting my time, but at that time I really needed some type of outlet. Therapy was the outlet given to me, but it was not working.

Time went on and it got worse (in therapy and my life). I hated my foster parents and my sister was getting in trouble. Mommy got sicker and my father stopped coming by.

I tried to make the best of things. Sometimes I'd be my regular happy self, doing my thing and chilling. But other times I'd get upset. I would throw stuff out the window and watch it smash, or I'd cry real hard. My tantrums would only last a few minutes, but they'd happen often. I just wanted everything back to the way it was.

**Every few weeks, she would not be there and I'd have to talk to some old geezer.**

A lot of the time I would stay to myself. I would sit in my room and think about all the things I would do if I were an adult and I could do whatever I wanted. Or I just wanted to be with my mommy and stay there, far away from reality's problems.

After eight or nine months, my second therapist left and I got a new one, and then I got a few more. Let's say I got a few too many (four or five in all). The more they changed, the more I hated therapy.

Then, one of them decided I was depressed. She told me, "Maybe we should try something." She wanted me to go on medication. She said it would help me have a "normal" attitude toward things.

I was 12 and at that age I was like, "What the hell did I do?" She asked me how I felt about going on the medication. I said I didn't want to take it, but she told me it was mandatory. I felt like I had no rights at all.

The whole thing seemed so unreal, and I didn't know how

it would be, so in the end I just said, "Yeah, whatever." If I kept protesting, I didn't think it would matter. My mom told the therapist that she didn't want me on medication, but they put me on it anyway.

The first drug they put me on was Wellbutrin. I took it once a day, and my foster mother would check my mouth every time to make sure I'd swallowed it. For me, the side effects of Wellbutrin were sleeplessness, headaches, and nausea.

I could not sleep at night at all. Instead, I would play with my toys or read my books. I would think, "I sure hope I don't turn into a potato tonight." I'd also get sick to my stomach almost every other day for up to an hour.

Then, after taking the drug for a while, I felt my moods begin to change. I'd get hyper and then I'd feel low. I told my doctor. She said, "That's OK. That's the way it is," or something. But eventually I guess she heard what I had to say because after about a year she took me off that drug and put me on some different ones.

She put me on Lithium and Prozac, which are stronger drugs. I remember my doctor saying it was going to help me be "OK." This time I asked, "Is this mandatory?"

She said, "Well, I feel that you should be on it because of this in your life and that in your life." Basically she was telling me that it was mandatory. I was used to being a good girl so once again I thought, "OK, I'll take it," even though I didn't want to.

I took both drugs three times a day. I felt like my moods were no longer my own. I felt like they were trying to turn me into their robot.

For a little while of almost every day I would be out of it, like Alice down the rabbit hole. I would be low, just cut off from things. Then the roller coaster would go up and I'd be crazy, like I'd just drunk a million gallons of coffee and was going to the stars. I felt like I had two heads with different personalities.

I felt so different from before. Sometimes I really did feel happier. But when I was low, I felt so low I didn't even have the energy to cry. Then I felt lost in an endless cycle of regret. My main regret was that I had ever opened up to anyone.

I saw my psychiatrist every few weeks, and I told her I didn't want to be on the medication. I told her it was nasty. A few times they changed the dosage, but usually the psychiatrist just said I should keep taking them and they'd make me feel better.

By then, my foster mother trusted me and didn't check whether I was swallowing the pills nearly as much, so I began to hide them or throw them away any chance I got. I ditched the drugs about every other day. That probably made the drugs do even weirder things to me. But at the time, I felt like no one was listening to my protests, so that was my only way.

> **I said I didn't want to take medication, but she told me it was mandatory. I felt like I had no rights at all.**

I was on those drugs for almost two years. Eventually, they sent me to a residential treatment center in upstate New York, where I live now, because the therapists decided that that would be best. When I got here, I did not like it. You can't go anywhere unless you are on a special level. We do not have our own rooms. Back then I didn't even have a radio so I couldn't listen to music (talk about pissed).

But I did get off all the medication that I'd been put on and the doctor who took me off them said it had been unnecessary to put me on them in the first place. He said that I didn't act depressed. That, my friend, was a beautiful thing.

I've been off medication for about a year, and I don't ever want to be on them again. I know that some kids are helped by medication, but I also believe that sometimes kids are put on them when they shouldn't be, mainly because there just isn't anyone who knows how to help them open up and deal with their problems emotionally.

I also know from my own experience how important it is,

when you are taking medication, to have someone who you're sure will take your feelings seriously. Then if something doesn't feel right, you can tell that person and that person will help you.

After the experiences I've had with therapy and medication, I'm not sure I will ever really trust a therapist again. But I still say my first therapist was off the hook. She didn't treat me like a lab animal. She was real and upfront and helped me out. She was a real outlet for me. I believe that's really what I needed.

---

*Gloria was 17 when she wrote this story.*

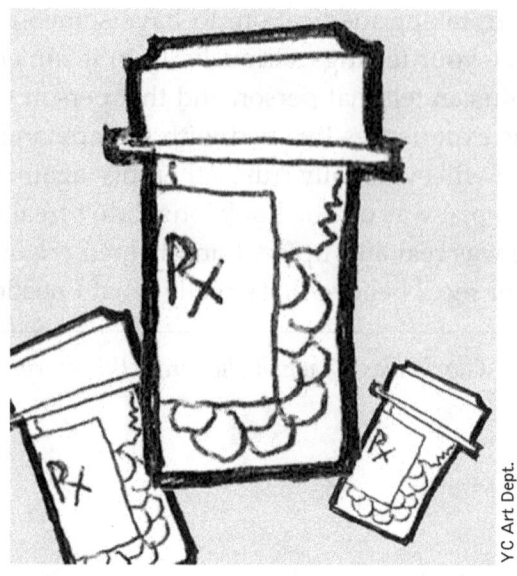

# What Are Anti-Depressants?

### By Carolyn Glaser

*Carolyn Glaser, a therapist who works with teens in New York City, explains how anti-depressants work.*

Anti-depressants aren't happy pills and they won't make a person happy, they'll just make you able to function, get out of bed and handle the day. I've seen teens go on anti-depressants and it helps them relax, sleep, not be as anxious.

I don't like it for a young person to be told that they have to be on anti-depressants. But I also think that there's a lot of resistance because there's a lot of misconceptions about anti-depressants.

A lot of people think anti-depressants will make you an addict or they'll make you all spacey. A lot of people think taking medication is a sign of weakness. They think you should be able to handle your own problems. But often depression is something that you can't help. It's like taking asthma medication if you have asthma. You need that medication to maintain yourself. If you've always had depression, I can't imagine why you wouldn't try it.

Anti-depressant medication is not an exact science, though, and sometimes you have to try a few different medications or different doses before you get it right. Kids may experience a numb feeling or other side effects, like nausea or sleeplessness, so anti-depressants have to be closely monitored and there has to be good communication between the doctors and the patient. You have to ask a kid if the medication is helpful. The kid can say if it's not. Then the drug has to be changed or the dosage adjusted.

# Inside A Psychiatrist's Head

### By Gloria Williams

We interviewed Dr. Leon Hoffman, a psychiatrist who treats people of all ages, in his Manhattan office. On our way there, I felt intimidated because I'd had so many bad experiences with therapists, but I found out he was a pretty cool guy. He was up front about the pros and cons of medication and therapy. He even said that therapists make mistakes. He said they're not mind readers, and that they rely on their patients being as honest as possible. I was impressed with his honesty. Here's what he had to say.

**Q: When should medication be prescribed and when shouldn't it be?**

**A:** There are some situations when medication is absolutely necessary, and other situations when it's overused.

If someone is in a severe emotional state, they aren't going to be able to address their real problems. Then the goal of prescribing medication is to help that person be more in control of their feelings. If you take medication and the depression gets a little better, maybe you can find a better way of dealing with the depressing situation. That's where therapy can help.

But some doctors do over-prescribe medication. Sometimes it's easier to give a child a pill than talk to that child. My philosophy is that with most cases, it's important not just to be on a pill. It's important to talk to someone about your problems.

**Q: All of us act strangely sometimes, but that doesn't mean everyone should be on medication. How do you judge if someone should be?**

**A:** What you evaluate is a person's relationships and how they're coping with life in general. Does that person have friends? How do they function in school? How are they getting along with their family? If your depression becomes so severe that it's interfering with your interactions, or if you become suicidal, for instance, then medication is needed.

**Q: Some of us take medication but don't like how it feels. What should our doctors do?**

**A:** Sometimes you can change the dosage. Sometimes you have to switch the medication. It's very important to be followed by a doctor for any unforeseen things that happen.

**Q: When I was on medication, I would get zoned out, and it still happens sometimes now that I'm not on medication. Why is that?**

**A:** It's very important to realize that people get zoned out for all kinds of reasons. People may get zoned out from medication. But they can also get zoned out from unpleasant feelings. So it's important not to automatically blame everything you're feeling on the medication.

# Analyze This!

**Q: What should you do if you're upset about your medication, but your doctor doesn't seem to be listening to you?**

**A:** I think the best thing to do is to try to speak to a different doctor in the same clinic or the same institution.

**Q: What do you do if your patients are having a problem with you?**

**A:** I try to help them understand. I try to understand if it's something that I'm doing. I encourage my patients to be as open as possible with their thoughts, even if they think I'm going to feel criticized. We're not mind readers. We rely on the patient trying to be as honest as possible. Still, sometimes people say, "I'm not going to see you anymore."

**Q: A lot of us in care are forced to go to therapy and take medication, so we don't trust the doctors. What can be done about that?**

**A:** How do you get help from a system when you don't fully trust the system? That's a very good question. I think somehow you have to begin talking within the system about how to address that problem.

---

*Gloria was 17 when she conducted this interview.*
*Jackie Knight, Shawn Fred, and Kareem Banks*
*also participated in the interview.*

# Crazy for Psychology

### By Erica Pierre

One night when I was 13 and still living in Haiti, I was lying in bed, thinking about what my life would be like in 20 years. My father wanted me to become a pediatrician. He was a lawyer, teacher, and school principal, but as a child, he'd wanted to be a doctor.

Life circumstances had prevented him from achieving his dream, and now he wanted me to achieve it for him. But as I lay in bed, all I could think was that I wanted a job I would enjoy. Suddenly, I got it. I wanted to become a psychologist.

I'd gone to see a psychologist a year earlier, when I was 12. I'd been having migraine headaches since I was 9 and nothing seemed to help. A doctor suggested the headaches might be psychosomatic (when a mental issue affects you physically) and sent me to a psychologist.

# Analyze This!

Dr. Joan, the psychologist, asked me a lot of questions. She asked how I felt about my family members, if I'd been in love, how I was doing in school. I thought that she could know everything about me just by asking questions, and it scared me. So at first I acted rude. I'd answer her with a yes or no even when it wasn't a yes or no question. I didn't tell her what was really on my mind, like how I felt uncertain and depressed about my future.

One day, I was upset because my grandma had wrongfully accused me of breaking the living room window. That afternoon Dr. Joan asked me gently, "Well, Erica, how was your week?"

She seemed to notice that something was wrong. I hated that I couldn't hide anything from her. "Do I have to tell you every single thing happening in my life?" I said.

"Well, if there's something you want me to know, it's OK if you want to tell me," she said softly.

> **I thought that she could know everything about me just by asking questions, and it scared me.**

She was so damn nice it got on my nerves. "What the hell is wrong with you?" I said. "Why are you talking like I'm retarded?"

Instead of getting mad, Dr. Joan calmly took advantage of my outburst to try to help me deal with my anger better. She explained how I could react differently when I'm mad. She suggested that I talk to the person who upset me to get a better understanding of how they feel and why they've behaved the way they have.

I thought what she said made sense. I tried everything she suggested and it helped me to get along better with people. After that, I was fascinated by the way Dr. Joan thought. I was amazed that she found a way to know many things about me without me having to reveal them to her.

I wanted to know more about people, too. And I wanted to have that self-control that Dr. Joan appeared to have. I began asking her more about her job. She didn't mind explaining to me how she had become interested in psychology, what she liked about her job, and what her fears were.

Then I told a friend that I was interested in psychology, and she brought me a book her father had, called *The Power of Psychoanalysis*. It was full of stories about how people behaved in different circumstances, and how the desire to be important is stronger than sexual desire. I was fascinated.

That was the first of many psychology books I read. I discovered myself while reading these books. They helped me understand myself better, and I learned that I wasn't the only person who could benefit from therapy. Many other people needed help, and I wanted to help them.

One day, I went to my friend Leila's house to watch a movie that she loved. It was about a girl who committed suicide because her boyfriend cheated on her. The movie portrayed the girl like a brave heroine. But I told Leila that I didn't think the character was brave and that suicide was a cowardly act.

Leila asked, "If I were this girl, what would you think of me?"

"Are you telling me that you want to kill yourself?" I shouted.

After about 15 seconds she said, "Well, I don't know." But the look in her eyes told me everything. Then she exploded, "My parents expect too much from me and my father doesn't even care about me. He leaves the house to go to his mistress. I fail in everything I'm trying to do." She confessed that she was planning to do it the week after New Year's.

I listened carefully to everything she was saying without interrupting her. When I was sure she was done, I began talking. "Leila, you know that I love you and I'm sure your parents love you as well. If you commit suicide, many people are going to suffer. You represent the world for some people and I know you know it."

Afterward, I called her every day to see how she was doing. Looking back, I realize I probably should have asked an adult

## Analyze This!

for help. But luckily, Leila abandoned her suicidal idea, and I was relieved that I'd been able to help her. I felt like I'd saved my friend's life. But it wasn't until a month later when I was lying in bed thinking about my future that I realized I wanted to help people for a living.

In the morning I was so excited to announce to my family that I knew exactly what career I wanted when I grew up. Their reaction wasn't what I expected.

First I went to my grandma. "Mami, yesterday night I was thinking. I think that I want to become a psychologist."

She laughed and looked at me. "You have something bothering you," she said.

"No, I feel great," I said.

"Then why do you want to become a psychologist? Those people are crazy. They all have mental problems. That's why they become psychologists."

I didn't understand. I wasn't crazy. I just wanted to help others face and work through their emotional problems. I wanted to know what happens in people's minds, what makes them so alike and at the same time so different. I thought that maybe my grandma just couldn't understand these things because she was getting old. But my father reacted the same way. And at school, my teacher said, "You can't even deal with your problems. How do you think you're going to resolve other people's issues? After the therapy they'd be crazier than they were before!"

> **I wanted to help others face and work through their emotional problems.**

I felt so disappointed. It was supposed to be great news. They were supposed to say, "That's great, go for it!" But everybody I talked to thought that being a psychologist meant that you must have problems yourself. I began to wonder if my grandma, father and teacher were right. They were older and more experienced than me. What if it was true that I wanted to become a psychologist just to figure out or avoid my own problems?

I tried to give up on my dream. I discouraged myself by thinking about the many years it would take me to get a bachelor's degree, a master's degree, and then a Ph.D. in psychology.

But I couldn't stop reading books about psychology. Over the past four years, I've become more knowledgeable about how people think and feel. I've learned to tell people what they need to hear so that they feel accepted and comfortable with me. Recently, I quietly decided that psychology really was right for me, no matter what anyone says.

I realize now that the people who discouraged me saw emotional problems as something shameful. They seemed to think that only a weak person needs psychological help. But life is full of daily obstacles, and not everybody can handle them alone. All a psychologist does is help identify problems and offer help solving them. I don't think that people can solve their problems by ignoring them.

Having people discourage me challenged me to really question myself about what I wanted to do. Their opinions almost cost me my dream. But in the end, they only made me feel more strongly about my future career.

---

*Erica wrote this story when she was 19.*

# The Therapy Stigma

### By Erica Pierre

When I decided I wanted to be a psychologist, many people discouraged me. It seemed like there was a stigma about therapy and I wondered if that was particular to the black community that I come from. I decided to interview Dr. Alvin Poussaint, professor of psychiatry at Harvard Medical School and a well-known expert on mental health in the black community.

**Q: In general, what does the black community think about therapy?**

**A:** There's a stigma attached to mental illness in America as a whole, among people of all ethnicities. There's a joke that psychologists and psychiatrists are crazy themselves. Ridiculing the people who are delivering the care is a way of avoiding facing up to one's own mental problems.

The stigma seems to be a little bit higher among African-Americans because they tend to view mental illness as something to hide. Some of that is because of history. In the past, blacks were more likely to be sent to state hospitals and locked up against their will. They can't do that anymore, but I think there's still some fear of being put away without your permission.

**Q: Why do some people see mental illness as shameful?**

**A:** Instead of seeing it as an illness that you can get because of a chemical imbalance or from stress, they tend to see it as a defect in themselves. They feel that other people will see them as weak.

**Q: Does the stigma exist in black communities in other countries (like Haiti, where I'm from) or only in the American black community?**

**A:** In most cultures there's some stigma about "going crazy." I've traveled in Africa, China and the Caribbean and I think there's a stigma there as well. But what is seen as mental illness may vary in different cultures. If you're in Haiti and you hear voices, some people might not think that's a problem, if those people practice voodoo. But if you're hearing voices in the U.S., people might consider that a mental illness.

**Q: I once heard someone say that "black people don't go to therapists, they go to church." What do you think about that?**

**A:** That's not entirely true. A lot of black people go to therapy. But a large portion of the black community will seek out ministers and the church to deal with emotional problems. A lot of the time it probably helps because they're talking about it and seeking help. But ministers have to know when to refer certain people who are very ill to psychologists or psychiatrists.

**Q: I've heard that black people usually don't trust white therapists. Is that true?**

**A:** It varies. Some black people don't trust that a white therapist is going to be able to help them, and they'd prefer to go to a black therapist. White patients are the same way. A lot of patients prefer to go to a psychologist or psychiatrist who comes from the same culture. But black patients may fear not just that they won't be understood, but that a white therapist may be prejudiced and they won't get good care.

**Q: Do we need more black therapists in the U.S.?**

**A:** Absolutely. Black patients are likely to have a therapist of a different background than them. Even in a city like Boston, where I live, there are very few black therapists.

A black psychiatrist can make black patients feel a greater trust and feel more welcome. The other thing a black psychologist or psychiatrist can do is help educate and give a cultural perspective to the non-black therapists at their clinic who are treating black patients.

**Q: What can be done to eliminate the therapy stigma?**

**A:** People in medicine, public health associations and the U.S. Surgeon General all have to keep saying that there shouldn't be a stigma associated with being mentally ill. Mental illness is a disease like diabetes or hypertension. It's treatable with therapy and medication, and there's no need to suffer or not seek help because people feel it's a weakness. We have to encourage people not to stigmatize the mentally ill, not to make fun of them, not to abuse them, but to treat everyone with dignity and respect.

---

*Erica was 19 when she conducted this interview.*

# Walking Away From the Fight

### By Anonymous

One day about a year ago, my dad and I were driving through an unfamiliar neighborhood somewhere in suburban New Jersey. I'd told my dad where to turn, but he'd ignored me, and now he refused to admit that was why we were lost. As usual, our disagreement escalated into a huge fight.

"You have such serious problems!" he yelled. "You have so many issues I don't even know what to do with you."

"Just leave me alone!" I shouted. I hated that arguments with my dad could never be about just one thing. He seemed to see each fight as an opportunity to remind me of everything I'd ever done that he didn't like. He talked in absolutes—I always did this wrong, I never did that right. It felt like our relationship was just one big fight we kept coming back to over and over again.

"You need to be in therapy!" he yelled. "You're disturbed,

and you need to get some therapy and work on your issues!" He violently jerked the car into reverse, attempting to execute a three-point turn at the bottom of the dead-end street where we'd somehow ended up.

I started sobbing. I wanted to jump out of the car and run away. My dad's words made me feel like all the problems in our relationship were my fault, that there was something wrong with me that had to be fixed before I could be the daughter he wanted.

He made it sound like a therapist was an auto mechanic who'd pop open the hood and tweak something in my brain so that I would run smoothly. Then my dad would drive off into the sunset, and we'd live happily ever after.

My mom tells me my dad wasn't always like this. He used to be artistic, spontaneous, patient, and even fun, she says. I can hardly believe that the avid photographer who traveled across Europe by bicycle was my dad. The dad I know is gruff, short-tempered, and constantly fretting over money and his job.

He's been that way since I was 2, when he developed a rare disease called transverse myelitis (TM). TM damages the myelin sheath, the protective coating around the spinal cord. It can be fatal, and survivors are left with nerve damage that can cause paralysis, fatigue, and chronic pain.

My dad survived, but one of his hands was left stiff and useless, and he was often in pain. He managed these problems with physical therapy and daily medication, and eventually no noticeable physical signs of his illness remained. But those who are close to him know it changed him.

He became completely engrossed in his work and spent most of his time at his office in the city. When he came home to Westchester in the evening, I barely saw him. I'd hear his car pull up in the driveway and wonder if I had enough time to run to my room.

The front door would open, and Dad would call, "I'm home!"

If we didn't respond quickly enough, he'd start yelling that no one in this family cared about him enough to greet him after a long, hard day at work. Even if we called out "Hello!" as soon as he opened the door, he'd still find something to be angry about. "Why is the mail never on the front hall table?" he'd bluster. "Why is the kitchen always such a mess?"

My mom would say his name in a tired voice, but he'd cut her off with more complaints. Then he'd stomp upstairs to lie down.

I hated having to play out this same scene, night after night. On the one hand, I knew why he was yelling. Traveling on a crowded, stuffy train for nearly an hour made him feel ill and achy. I knew I should forgive him because I didn't really know how he felt, and if I were in his place, I might be angry too. But I still felt like shouting, "It's not fair! I didn't do anything to you!"

*I couldn't quite believe that I was supposed to tell some guy I'd never met before all sorts of personal information.*

My mom must have felt the same way, because she'd often snap back in response to each of his criticisms. Then the kitchen door would slam shut, signaling that their "discussion" was about to explode into a full-out fight.

My parents finally separated when I was almost 16, and I felt such relief. I thought that reduced tension between my parents would help my own relationship with my dad. But instead of making things easier, the divorce made things harder.

I was used to rarely spending time with my dad, but now my sister and I had to go to his house every week. Before, when my dad and I fought, my mom would step in and attempt to defuse the situation. Now I had to face him alone.

A few weeks after the fight in the car, my mom tentatively suggested it might help me to "talk to someone." I told her I wanted no part of it. After all, according to my dad, therapy was only for the "disturbed." If I went to therapy, it would prove him right. Besides, any problems I did have were nobody's business. I didn't need anyone's help.

But part of me almost wished my mom would force me into therapy. I wanted to get help without having to ask for it. I was overwhelmed by anger, sadness and self-doubt. Sometimes, without warning, I'd feel like I couldn't breathe and that I didn't exist, or the world didn't exist. It was like I'd suddenly been dropped into a bad dream. I'd want to run around and shout to make myself wake up and come back to the world, but I'd feel frozen in place. These occurrences made me feel isolated and scared.

> **Not everything was fine, and I was allowed to say so.**

Other times I was filled with contempt for myself. I was just another melodramatic suburban teenager who hated school and whose parents were getting divorced. My problems seemed trivial. A therapist probably wouldn't want to waste her time on me.

Then, about a week after my mom's suggestion, I started talking to a close friend about how I was feeling. She told me that she used to suffer from severe social anxiety. When she was 13, it got so bad that she couldn't go to school, and she barely left her house for a year. I was surprised to hear this. My friend sometimes seemed shy compared to loud, outgoing me, but I never would've guessed that at once time she couldn't even go out to see a movie.

She told me that she could identify with how I was feeling and that it sounded like I might be having panic attacks. I hesitantly told her I was thinking of seeing a therapist, unsure of how she'd react.

"I can give you the name of mine if you want," she said. "He's really good."

I thanked her and said I'd think about it.

After that, my mind was made up. I told my mom that I wanted to talk to someone after all. She made an appointment for me with Jim (not his real name), a psychotherapist who was doing my parents' divorce mediation.

I came to the first meeting not knowing what to expect. I couldn't quite believe that I was supposed to tell some guy I'd never met before all sorts of personal information about my life. I was scared that after I'd told him all about the stuff between my dad and me, he would tell me that my dad was right, that I was the problem and everything was my fault. Nervously, I sat down on the scratchy couch in Jim's office, my eyes on the floor.

"How are you?" he asked me.

"Fine, thanks," I told him, without thinking.

"Are you really?" he asked. "Is everything really fine?"

I was surprised. This was the first time that I felt like someone who'd asked me how I was actually wanted to know the truth. Not everything was fine, and I was allowed to say so.

I've been seeing Jim once a week for almost a year now. Each week, I've become more comfortable opening up and telling him what I'm going through. He's a good listener, and he gives me advice on how to deal with my dad. One of the most important things I've learned is that I can't always control the situation I'm in, but I can control how I respond to it.

The easy reaction in any conflict is to let my emotions take over, leaving me angry and hurt. The difficult reaction is to stop and think about why the other person is acting the way they are, and then choose not to get upset. It takes work, but I do my best to use this technique when I find myself in a conflict with my dad. Although it's not a perfect system, it has helped me a lot.

On a recent Tuesday night, my mom dropped my younger sister and me off at my dad's house for dinner. Dad wasn't home yet, and neither of us had thought to bring our keys, so we sat down on the step to wait for him. After 20 minutes, his car rolled into the driveway. He got out, slamming the door behind him, and strode over to us.

"What are you doing out here?" he asked gruffly. He dug

around in his coat pocket, pulled out his key and jammed it in the lock.

"Well, you were late, and we didn't have a key—" I began.

"Oh, so it's my fault is it? Everything's always Dad's fault around here, right? Well maybe if you'd been responsible enough to have your key with you, this wouldn't have happened."

I looked down at my sister, but, as usual, she kept her mouth shut and looked away. "I'm sorry Dad," I tried to explain. "It's just that it's in my other bag, and I didn't think I'd need it since you're usually home when we get here. I mean, I'm assuming you ended up taking a later train…"

My dad jiggled the key back and forth impatiently, trying not to drop his briefcase and overcoat. "What train I take is not the issue here! You need to start taking a little responsibility for once in your life instead of always making me the bad guy." The door opened with a click, and we all stumbled into the house.

> **Therapy isn't magic. It doesn't necessarily make things better for you; it gives you the tools to make things better for yourself.**

I was starting to get really mad now. I wanted to shout, "I need to take responsibility? Look who's talking! You're the one who always blames things on other people!" Then I stopped and took a breath. "This is not about me," I said to myself. "This is about Daddy being tired and the train being too hot. This is about him being stressed and having a headache. This is not about me."

"I'm sorry for anything I've done to make you feel that way," I said carefully. "I'm also sorry if you're not feeling well tonight. I'm going to go work on some homework now, but let me know if you need any help with dinner."

As I walked down the hallway and shut my door behind me, I could hear Dad yelling about who did I think I was to walk away from him in the middle of a discussion like that and how I was shutting him out of my life by refusing to communicate with him.

Although I wanted to run out of my room and tell him he had it all wrong, I took a book out of my backpack instead. I decided not to let him draw me into an argument that would accomplish nothing more than both of us yelling at each other for a while.

That night, at the dinner table, my dad suddenly turned to me. "I'm sorry I got mad at you earlier, but I wasn't feeling well," he said quickly.

I groaned inwardly. My dad is a notorious "sorry but-er." To me, "sorry buts" are less apologies than excuses. But I could see that it was difficult for my dad to say even this much, so I said, "OK," and we all went back to quietly eating our spaghetti.

My dad and I may always have a difficult relationship. Therapy isn't magic. It doesn't necessarily make things better for you; it gives you the tools to make things better for yourself. Some days I wish I would never see my dad again, and other days I wish we were closer.

My dad and I are different in many ways. Our opinions clash on everything from national politics to my frequently unmade bed, and many of our fights stem from these differences. But I think our fights escalate because of our similarities. We both like to feel in control, and we can be very stubborn. If we both act the way we're naturally inclined then we become stuck in an ongoing cycle of conflict. These standoffs can only end when one of us changes the way we respond to the other.

I hope that someday my dad will stop seeing therapy as a negative thing because I think it might help him to learn about the choices he can make in his own life. But I realize that I can't change him. Instead, with work and help, I'm changing myself by learning a different way to respond to conflict than the one he taught me. I'm creating one more difference between my dad and me, but this one might actually end fights instead of start them.

---

*The author was in high school when she wrote this story.*

## FICTION SPECIAL

# Lost and Found

Darcy Wills winced at the loud rap music coming from her sister's room.

    My rhymes were rockin'
    MC's were droppin'
    People shoutin' and hip-hoppin'
    Step to me and you'll be inferior
    'Cause I'm your lyrical superior.

Darcy went to Grandma's room. The darkened room smelled of lilac perfume, Grandma's favorite, but since her stroke Grandma did not notice it, or much of anything.

"Bye, Grandma," Darcy whispered from the doorway. "I'm going to school now."

Just then, the music from Jamee's room cut off, and Jamee rushed into the hallway.

---

The teen characters in the Bluford novels, a fiction series by Townsend Press, struggle with many of the same difficult issues as the writers in this book. Here's the first chapter from *Lost and Found*, by Anne Schraff, the first book in the series. In this novel, high school sophomore Darcy contends with the return of her long-absent father, the troubling behavior of her younger sister Jamee, and the beginning of her first relationship.

## Analyze This!

"Like she even hears you," Jamee said as she passed Darcy. Just two years younger than Darcy, Jamee was in eighth grade, though she looked older.

"It's still nice to talk to her. Sometimes she understands. You want to pretend she's not here or something?"

"She's not," Jamee said, grabbing her backpack.

"Did you study for your math test?" Darcy asked. Mom was an emergency room nurse who worked rotating shifts. Most of the time, Mom was too tired to pay much attention to the girls' schoolwork. So Darcy tried to keep track of Jamee.

"Mind your own business," Jamee snapped.

"You got two D's on your last report card," Darcy scolded. "You wanna flunk?" Darcy did not want to sound like a nagging parent, but Jamee wasn't doing her best. Maybe she couldn't make A's like Darcy, but she could do better.

Jamee stomped out of the apartment, slamming the door behind her. "Mom's trying to get some rest!" Darcy yelled. "Do you have to be so selfish?" But Jamee was already gone, and the apartment was suddenly quiet.

Darcy loved her sister. Once, they had been good friends. But now all Jamee cared about was her new group of rowdy friends. They leaned on cars outside of school and turned up rap music on their boom boxes until the street seemed to tremble like an earthquake. Jamee had even stopped hanging out with her old friend Alisha Wrobel, something she used to do every weekend.

Darcy went back into the living room, where her mother sat in the recliner sipping coffee. "I'll be home at 2:30, Mom," Darcy said. Mom smiled faintly. She was tired, always tired. And lately she was worried too. The hospital where she worked was cutting staff. It seemed each day fewer people were expected to do more work. It was like trying to climb a mountain that keeps getting taller as you go. Mom was forty-four, but just yesterday she said, "I'm like an old car that's run out of warranty, baby. You know what happens then. Old car is ready for the junk heap. Well, maybe that hospital is gonna tell me one of these days—'Mattie Mae Wills, we don't need you anymore. We can get somebody younger and cheaper.'"

"Mom, you're not old at all," Darcy had said, but they were only words, empty words. They could not erase the dark, weary lines from beneath her mother's eyes.

Darcy headed down the street toward Bluford High School. It was not a terrible neighborhood they lived in; it just was not good. Many front yards were not cared for. Debris—fast food wrappers, plastic bags, old newspapers—blew around and piled against fences and curbs. Darcy hated that. Sometimes she and other kids from school spent Saturday mornings cleaning up, but it seemed a losing battle. Now, as she walked, she tried to focus on small spots of beauty along the way. Mrs. Walker's pink and white roses bobbed proudly in the morning breeze. The Hustons' rock garden was carefully designed around a wooden windmill.

As she neared Bluford, Darcy thought about the science project that her biology teacher, Ms. Reed, was assigning. Darcy was doing hers on tidal pools. She was looking forward to visiting a real tidal pool, taking pictures, and doing research. Today, Ms. Reed would be dividing the students into teams of two. Darcy wanted to be paired with her close friend, Brisana Meeks. They were both excellent students, a cut above most kids at Bluford, Darcy thought.

"Today, we are forming project teams so that each student can gain something valuable from the other," Ms. Reed said as Darcy sat at her desk. Ms. Reed was a tall, stately woman who reminded Darcy of the Statue of Liberty. She would have been a perfect model for the statue if Lady Liberty had been a black woman. She never would have been called pretty, but it was possible she might have been called a handsome woman. "For this assignment, each of you will be working with someone you've never worked with before."

Darcy was worried. If she was not teamed with Brisana,

# Analyze This!

maybe she would be teamed with some really dumb student who would pull her down. Darcy was a little ashamed of herself for thinking that way. Grandma used to say that all flowers are equal, but different. The simple daisy was just as lovely as the prize rose. But still Darcy did not want to be paired with some weak partner who would lower her grade.

"Darcy Wills will be teamed with Tarah Carson," Ms. Reed announced.

Darcy gasped. Not Tarah! Not that big, chunky girl with the brassy voice who squeezed herself into tight skirts and wore lime green or hot pink satin tops and cheap jewelry. Not Tarah who hung out with Cooper Hodden, that loser who was barely hanging on to his football eligibility. Darcy had heard that Cooper had been left back once or twice and even got his driver's license as a sophomore. Darcy's face felt hot with anger. Why was Ms. Reed doing this?

Hakeem Randall, a handsome, shy boy who sat in the back row, was teamed with the class blabbermouth, LaShawn Appleby. Darcy had a secret crush on Hakeem since freshman year. So far she had only shared this with her diary, never with another living soul.

It was almost as though Ms. Reed was playing some devilish game. Darcy glanced at Tarah, who was smiling broadly. Tarah had an enormous smile, and her teeth contrasted harshly with her dark red lipstick. "Great," Darcy muttered under her breath.

Ms. Reed ord e red the teams to meet so they could begin to plan their projects.

As she sat down by Tarah, Darcy was instantly sickened by a syrupy-sweet odor.

*She must have doused herself with cheap perfume this morning ,* Darcy thought.

"Hey, girl," Tarah said. "Well, don't you look down in the mouth. What's got you lookin' that way?"

It was hard for Darcy to meet new people, especially someone like Tarah, a person Aunt Charlotte would call "low class." These were people who were loud and rude. They drank too much, used drugs, got into fights and ruined the neighborhood. They yelled ugly insults at people, even at their friends. Darcy did not actually know that Tarah did anything like this personally, but she seemed like the type who did.

"I just didn't think you'd be interested in tidal pools," Darcy explained.

Tarah slammed her big hand on the desk, making her gold bracelets jangle like ice cubes in a glass, and laughed. Darcy had never heard a mule bray, but she was sure it made exactly the same sound. Then Tarah leaned close and whispered, "Girl, I don't know a tidal pool from a fool. Ms. Reed stuck us together to mess with our heads, you hear what I'm sayin'?"

"Maybe we could switch to other partners," Darcy said nervously.

A big smile spread slowly over Tarah's face. "Nah, I think I'm gonna enjoy this. You're always sittin' here like a princess collecting your A's. Now you gotta work with a regular person, so you better loosen up, girl!"

Darcy felt as if her teeth were glued to her tongue. She fumbled in her bag for her outline of the project. It all seemed like a horrible joke now. She and Tarah Carson standing knee-deep in the muck of a tidal pool!

"Worms live there, don't they?" Tarah asked, twisting a big gold ring on her chubby finger.

"Yeah, I guess," Darcy replied.

"Big green worms," Tarah continued. "So if you get your feet stuck in the bottom of that old tidal pool, and you can't get out, do the worms crawl up your clothes?"

Darcy ignored the remark. "I'd like for us to go there soon, you know, look around."

"My boyfriend, Cooper, he goes down to the ocean all the time. He can take us. He says he's seen these fiddler crabs. They

## Analyze This!

look like big spiders, and they'll try to bite your toes off. Cooper says so," Tarah said.

"Stop being silly," Darcy shot back. "If you're not even going to be serious . . . "

"You think you're better than me, don't you?" Tarah suddenly growled.

"I never said—" Darcy blurted.

"You don't have to say it, girl. It's in your eyes. You think I'm a low-life and you're something special. Well, I got more friends than you got fingers and toes together. You got no friends, and everybody laughs at you behind your back. Know what the word on you is? Darcy Wills give you the chills."

Just then, the bell rang, and Darcy was glad for the excuse to turn away from Tarah, to hide the hot tears welling in her eyes. She quickly rushed from the classroom, relieved that school was over. Darcy did not think she could bear to sit through another class just now.

Darcy headed down the long street towards home. She did not like Tarah. Maybe it was wrong, but it was true. Still, Tarah's brutal words hurt. Even stupid, awful people might tell you the truth about yourself. And Darcy did not have any real friends, except for Brisana. Maybe the other kids were mocking her behind her back. Darcy was very slender, not as shapely as many of the other girls. She remembered the time when Cooper Hodden was hanging in front of the deli with his friends, and he yelled as Darcy went by, "Hey, is that really a female there? Sure don't look like it. Looks more like an old broomstick with hair. " His companions laughed rudely, and Darcy had walked a little faster.

A terrible thought clawed at Darcy. Maybe she was the loser, not Tarah. Tarah was always hanging with a bunch of kids, laughing and joking. She would go down the hall to the lockers and greetings would come from everywhere. "Hey, Tarah!" "What's up, Tar?" "See ya at lunch, girl." When Darcy went to the lockers, there was dead silence.

Darcy usually glanced into stores on her way home from school. She enjoyed looking at the trays of chicken feet and pork ears at the little Asian grocery store. Sometimes she would even steal a glance at the diners sitting by the picture window at the Golden Grill Restaurant. But today she stared straight ahead, her shoulders drooping.

If this had happened last year, she would have gone directly to Grandma's house, a block from where Darcy lived. How many times had Darcy and Jamee run to Grandma's, eaten applesauce cookies, drunk cider, and poured out their troubles to Grandma. Somehow, their problems would always dissolve in the warmth of her love and wisdom. But now Grandma was a frail figure in the corner of their apartment, saying little. And what little she did say made less and less sense.

Darcy was usually the first one home. The minute she got there, Mom left for the hospital to take the 3:00 to 11:00 shift in the ER. By the time Mom finished her paperwork at the hospital, she would be lucky to be home again by midnight. After Mom left, Darcy went to Grandma's room to give her the malted nutrition drink that the doctor ordered her to have three times a day.

"Want to drink your chocolate malt, Grandma?" Darcy asked, pulling up a chair beside Grandma's bed.

Grandma was sitting up, and her eyes were open. "No. I'm not hungry," she said listlessly. She always said that.

"You need to drink your malt, Grandma," Darcy insisted, gently putting the straw between the pinched lips.

Grandma sucked the malt slowly. "Grandma, nobody likes me at school," Darcy said. She did not expect any response. But there was a strange comfort in telling Grandma anyway. "Everybody laughs at me. It's because I'm shy and maybe stuck-up, too, I guess. But I don't mean to be. Stuck-up, I mean. Maybe I'm weird. I could be weird, I guess. I could be like Aunt Charlotte . . ." Tears rolled down Darcy's cheeks. Her heart ached

## Analyze This!

with loneliness. There was nobody to talk to anymore, nobody who had time to listen, nobody who understood.

Grandma blinked and pushed the straw away. Her eyes brightened as they did now and then. "You are a wonderful girl. Everybody knows that," Grandma said in an almost normal voice. It happened like that sometimes. It was like being in the middle of a dark storm and having the clouds part, revealing a patch of clear, sunlit blue. For just a few precious minutes, Grandma was bright-eyed and saying normal things.

"Oh, Grandma, I'm so lonely," Darcy cried, pressing her head against Grandma's small shoulder.

"You were such a beautiful baby," Grandma said, stroking her hair." 'That one is going to shine like the morning star.' That's what I told your Mama. 'That child is going to shine like the morning star.' Tell me, Angelcake, is your daddy home yet?"

Darcy straightened. "Not yet." Her heart pounded so hard, she could feel it thumping in her chest. Darcy's father had not been home in five years.

"Well, tell him to see me when he gets home. I want him to buy you that blue dress you liked in the store window. That's for you, Angelcake. Tell him I've got money. My social security came, you know. I have money for the blue dress," Grandma said, her eyes slipping shut.

Just then, Darcy heard the apartment door slam. Jamee had come home. Now she stood in the hall, her hands belligerently on her hips. "Are you talking to Grandma again?" Jamee demanded.

"She was talking like normal," Darcy said. "Sometimes she does. You know she does."

"That is so stupid," Jamee snapped. "She never says anything right anymore. Not anything!" Jamee's voice trembled.

Darcy got up quickly and set down the can of malted milk. She ran to Jamee and put her arms around her sister. "Jamee, I know you're hurting too."

"Oh, don't be stupid," Jamee protested, but Darcy hugged her more tightly, and in a few seconds Jamee was crying. "She was the best thing in this stupid house," Jamee cried. "Why'd she have to go?"

"She didn't go," Darcy said. "Not really."

"She did! She did!" Jamee sobbed. She struggled free of Darcy, ran to her room, and slammed the door. In a minute, Darcy heard the bone-rattling sound of rap music.

*Lost and Found, a Bluford Series™ novel, is reprinted with permission from Townsend Press. Copyright © 2002.*

---

Want to read more? This and other Bluford Series™ novels and paperbacks can be purchased for $1 each at www.townsendpress.com.

# A Teen Guide to Getting Help

It can be frustrating to need help for emotional or mental health problems and not understand what kind of help is available or where to find it. Therapy, the focus of this book, can be a major source of help. But as these stories show, there are many different kinds of therapy and therapists, and not all of them will be helpful to you. A big part of getting successful support to deal with a mental health problem is knowing what kind of help you need, what to expect, and how to speak up if you're not satisfied.

This guide is designed to help you get the services that are best for you. It covers some typical issues for which teens seek help. It also briefly describes the kinds of people who provide help. And it describes the type of help they provide and the ways they provide it. After reading this guide you may have more questions. Talk with friends and with an adult you trust.

### How Do I Know If I Need Help?

When people have a fever or a cold, they have a *physical* problem. Similarly, when people frequently feel sad, find it difficult to concentrate in school, or feel overwhelmed by life's daily problems, they have what is called an *emotional* problem. As with physical problems, emotional problems can be mild, such as occasional sadness, or severe, such as weeks or months of feeling low.

Just as some physical illnesses or injuries can be addressed through rest or physical therapy, emotional problems can be addressed through self-help, counseling, and various kinds of therapy. Emotional problems, like physical problems, can also be treated with medication. Some kinds of medication can help balance your body chemistry to help you feel more in control of your feelings—somewhat like how other drugs can attack germs and help restore the balance needed for physical health.

Many teens seek help for emotional problems that have official names—like sexual abuse or depression or bulimia. But there is also a more general area of "life problems" for which teens may need guidance and outside support. For example, if you are feeling grief over the loss of a loved one, or way too much anxiety about what the future may hold, you may not have a condition with a name, but you may still need help and support to work through the issue. Several of the approaches and kinds of professionals described here may be helpful in coping with a temporary "life problem."

So how do you know if you need to seek that kind of help?

We can try to answer this question by looking at depression. That's the name people often use to describe everything from occasional sad moods to a serious disease requiring medical treatment. People who are depressed can feel sad, discouraged, and hopeless. They can feel irritable, lose interest and pleasure in daily activities, and feel worthless and alone. They can feel very angry.

Many people experience these feelings from time to time. However, if you have those kinds of feelings for weeks or months on end—and if they make it hard for you to get out of bed in the morning, go out in public, enjoy eating, socialize with friends, or participate in other activities you think you really should be enjoying—you need to seek therapy (more on therapy below). The feelings will not just go away by themselves.

Even mild depression can lead to thoughts of suicide and actual suicide attempts. Again, many people have occasional thoughts of suicide when they are very upset, such as after breaking up with a boyfriend or girlfriend. But if you continue to think about hurting yourself and are planning ways to end your life, you must tell someone and get professional help. If you won't tell an adult, tell a peer. Start sharing your feelings with a trusted friend if this is easier for you.

But you don't have to be depressed or feel suicidal to seek help. There are many other problems that can affect your ability to function and be happy. You may have feelings of loneliness, anxiety, or isolation. Perhaps you have conflicts with parents, siblings, or friends, or maybe someone in your family is suffering from mental or physical illness. Maybe you can't concentrate enough in school to do as well as you know you can.

If you have a problem that is interfering with your ability to feel productive or deal with the daily ups and downs of life, your best option is to connect with someone who can help.

## Who Can Help Me? How Do I Know What Kind of Help Is Best For Me?

Professional therapy is not the only kind of help out there. In the next few paragraphs we'll briefly describe some other ways you can seek help for an emotional problem. Even if you're going to therapy, knowing how to use these other supports can be helpful. We start with the most informal kinds of counseling you can get, and work up to the most formal or specialized.

**Help yourself.** First, there's **self-help**. Self-help means what it sounds like. You help yourself, often without any counselor at all. If you feel sad or angry because you're shy and can't make friends, and you read a book or magazine article on how to be less shy, and you feel happier because it works, you're doing great. There's probably no need to go to a counselor.

If you're upset, you can try writing down your feelings in a journal and describing the circumstances that are causing you to feel that way. Writing can help you release feelings that are bottled up and may help you see things differently and find solutions to your problem.

**Get help from peers.** The next level is getting help from friends. There are two main ways to do that: informal help from people you know, and something more formal called **peer self-help.**

Informal help from your friends means talking to friends about your problems. If you're feeling lonely, angry, or sad, confiding in a friend can help you feel better (as it helped many of the writers in this book). You probably already know that, and already do it. Again, friends can help up to a certain point: if you feel the problem is serious, you many need more help than your friends can give.

Peer self-help is a more formal way of getting help from people like you. It usually happens in groups. The groups are often run (or "facilitated") by an adult professional, but the real benefit comes from other teens in the group. So, for example, if you are cutting and want to stop, you might be able to find a self-help group of teens whose problems led them to cut themselves. They get together regularly to talk about problems in their lives and what strategies they use to try to stop cutting.

**Get help from community members.** There are lots of people in your day-to-day life who may be helpful to you. They might include **school counselors, teachers, clergy, coaches, mentors,** and any other adult who you trust and feel comfortable talking to about your problems. Some of them, like a minister, may have some training in counseling. Others, like a mentor, may not. But you're a good judge of how comfortable you are talking to them. If you start to feel better after talking with them, great. If not, they may be able to recommend someone else who could be helpful. Remember, it may take more than one talk session to help you feel better about yourself and your life, so give yourself and your counselor a chance.

**Get help from professionals.** Therapists are professionals who are specially trained to help people with mental health issues. A therapist may be a psychiatrist, a psychologist, or a social worker.

But whatever their training and background, most therapists do pretty much the same thing. They listen closely to how you describe what's making you feel bad. Then they work with you to help you change the thinking or feelings or actions that cause you problems or pain.

# Analyze This!

## When They Say I Need Therapy or Counseling, What Do They Mean? What Kinds Are Available?

**Counseling** is a process where people explore their feelings, behavior, and what's going on in their lives. People go to counseling because they want to find ways to feel better and be more effective in their lives. (This kind of counseling is often called **therapy** or **psychotherapy**, or **psychological counseling** to show that it's different from something like job counseling.) If you get into formal counseling or therapy, you'll probably experience **individual therapy, group therapy,** or **family therapy,** or perhaps all of them. If your problems are severe, you may be **hospitalized**. We briefly describe these options below.

**Individual Therapy:** In individual therapy, you meet one-on-one with a counselor, usually at his or her office. You usually meet regularly, at least once a week, for anywhere from a few months to a year or longer, depending on the issues you're working on. You play an active role in defining the goals of your therapy with your counselor.

**Group Therapy:** In group therapy, a group of people who share common problems, concerns, and questions meet regularly to discuss feelings, and to listen to and support each other. For example, people who have lost loved ones may participate in bereavement groups. The groups are often (but not always) led by a mental health professional. Groups are also common in drug treatment programs. Everyone in the group has a drug problem, and the groups are often led by people who have their addictions under control, and who are especially skilled at working with people with drug problems.

Peer self-help groups are one kind of group counseling, and they exist for many, many issues. Alateen is a peer self-help group for teens who have family members with alcohol problems. There are peer groups for teen parents, teens with eating problems, teens who've lost a loved one, and for teens with many other issues.

**Family Therapy:** In family therapy, two or more members of a family will meet together and separately with a counselor to discuss conflicts, issues, and communication in the family. The counselor helps the family members deal with important issues without taking sides.

**Hospitalization:** If you have severe emotional or mental health problems, such as strong feelings of hopelessness or that you may hurt yourself or someone else, or that you're losing control, or that you cannot quit drugs without more structure and support, you may want to be hospitalized or referred to a drug rehab center. Hospitalization (which is also called "in-patient" treatment because you stay in the hospital) gives you a chance to get intensive services. For example, you may participate in individual, group, family, or peer counseling every day, as well as be given medication, to see what helps you most.

## What If I Feel Uncomfortable in Therapy?

One goal of therapy is to help you solve some problems, and to think differently about the problems you can't solve, so you can manage them better. When that happens, your self-esteem usually starts to rise. However, it can be very uncomfortable to look at problems in your life.

If you begin to feel uncomfortable in therapy, or feel that you are not making progress, don't just jump to another therapist. Discuss these issues with your therapist. A good therapist should be willing to talk with you about treatment issues, and about whether the therapy is meeting your needs. A good therapist should also be willing to consider changing the way he or she works with you.

It is usually a bad idea to make a snap decision concerning your therapist. It is important in therapy to gradually face hard issues about yourself or others in your life. That can be very difficult. Sometimes the *best* therapist is the one who is demanding and sometimes even makes you feel pretty uncomfortable. The times that you want "out" of therapy or feel you need another therapist may be when you're making the most progress. At those times, it can be hard to figure out whether you don't like the *therapist*, or whether you don't like the *issues* he or she is asking you to think about. You need to be able to trust that your therapist has your best interests at heart, even if he or she sometimes makes you feel uncomfortable.

It takes time to develop trust in a new relationship and to comfortably share feelings, so give your therapist and yourself some time. But if you've given it an honest shot and still don't feel you can trust your therapist, or if you don't feel like you're making progress over time, you may need a change.

### Can I Change Therapists?

Who you see for help should depend most on who you feel comfortable with and who is being most helpful to you. If you start with a therapist and either feel uncomfortable or feel that you are not making progress, or you are prescribed medication and don't want it, you need to discuss these issues with your therapist. Together you can decide whether it would be best for you to see another therapist or whether you need more time to work together.

It can be helpful, before starting therapy, to check out more than one therapist. If it's possible for you to do so, meet with two or three therapists, ask them how they work, and try to get a sense of how comfortable you feel with each.

But it may not be possible for you to "shop around." For example, you may be assigned a therapist. Yet even if you are assigned a therapist, you can ask to be changed to a new one if, after working together for a time, you feel that person is not right for you.

### Privacy

When you talk with someone about your private issues, you probably don't want them sharing that information without your permission. It's a good idea to ask the therapist in your first session what sort of confidentiality he or she can provide. For example, will the therapist share your conversations with your parents? With other people in the agency? Will the therapist share some kinds of information, but not others?

In general, people who offer licensed psychological counseling (psychiatrists, psychologists, and social workers) can offer much more confidentiality than informal counselors, like teachers and mentors (who may not be legally required to keep your conversations confidential). You need to ask them who they share information with and why—and then make your own decisions about what you want revealed to your parents and other concerned persons.

Note that even if everything else you say is confidential, therapists are obligated to tell others if you threaten to harm yourself or others.

### A Word About "Cognitive-Behavioral" Therapy

In addition to the forms of therapy described here (individual counseling, family counseling, etc.) there are many *kinds* of therapy. One kind that has been shown to work well with teens for some issues is cognitive-behavioral therapy. That's a fancy name for a pretty simple technique.

"Cognitive" means "thinking." In the first part of cognitive-behavioral therapy you work to replace self-defeating or self-destructive thoughts with more helpful thoughts. For example, if you're failing in school, you may think, "I'm sure to fail every class." But if you can change your *thinking* to, "I failed because I didn't study," and, "If I study for my next test, I may do better," then you're half way there to a good change.

But just changing your thinking isn't enough. You also have to change your behavior, which, of course, is what you do. In the example about failing classes, if you change your *behavior* too (that is, you actually do some studying)—then things will start to change for the better.

# Analyze This!

Therapists who use cognitive-behavioral methods help support you in changing negative thinking and actions into more positive approaches.

For more information about cognitive-behavioral therapy, read Megan Cohen's story ("Worried Sick" on p. 48) and La'Quesha Barner's interview ("Explaining Cognitive-Behavorial Therapy") on p. 53.

**A Word About Medication**

Just as doctors prescribe medication to treat physical illness, doctors also sometimes prescribe medication to treat emotional problems, such as depression.

There is medication for all kinds of emotional problems, but the most common ones for which teens get medication include depression, having trouble focusing (ADD, ADHD), and severe acting out or uncontrolled behavior (ODD).

One medication may be effective for some people but not for others. For example, many people use anti-depressants and feel the medication changed their lives by lifting their depression. But there are others for whom the medication has not worked as well. For teens, there's another issue. Studies show that for 2 or 3 teens out of 100 taking anti-depressants may actually make them feel more suicidal.

Also, if it is suggested that you take medication, you may wonder if it's because medication is cheaper than "talk therapy." Or maybe the clinic hasn't taken enough time to really evaluate you and they seem be jumping to the conclusion that you need medication. Or *you* may feel it is easier to take medication than to talk about your problems, so you go along, even though it might not seem like the best thing.

That's why you need to ask questions, and discuss your concerns with your therapist when you start any therapy program, especially one that involves medication. Medication may be necessary and very effective, but you and your therapist need to give careful thought to whether you need them.

And then, over time you, your therapist (and the psychiatrist who prescribed the medication) will evaluate the effectiveness of the drug and make changes until you figure out what works best. Your input will be very important because you are the only one who really knows how it is affecting you.

It is important to take medication exactly as prescribed, and then to notice how it makes you feel. If it doesn't seem to be working or has unpleasant side effects—or makes you feel suicidal—you may need to be put on another medication or get a smaller dose, or go off medication altogether. But since getting the right medication and the right dose to reduce your symptoms is complicated, it is very important that you work closely with your therapist and assigned psychiatrist.

You need to play an active role in coming up with a treatment plan that works for you, and in monitoring how the medication is affecting you.

Remember, some problems can be treated by self-help and informal counseling with adults you trust. But for other problems you may need help from therapists and sometimes from medication, or even hospitalization. Don't be afraid to seek help if you feel you need it. Seeking help early may prevent problems from becoming more severe.

# Mental Health Terms You May Want to Know

You may have heard many of these terms and be unsure of what they mean. This list is designed to make you more familiar with these terms, and to explain what they mean.

### Typical Emotional Issues Facing Teens

Following are brief descriptions of some of the more common emotional issues that teens experience:

**Depression** is the name people use to describe everything from occasional sad moods to a serious disease requiring medical treatment. Depression can be caused by chemical imbalances in your brain, or by traumatic events in your life, such as abuse, the loss of someone dear to you, or conflict with parents, teachers, or friends. People who are depressed can feel sad, discouraged, and hopeless. They can feel irritable, lose interest and pleasure in daily activities, and feel worthless and alone. If you have those kinds of feelings for weeks or months on end, you need to seek professional therapy from an adult.

Since the cause of depression can be complicated, it's often important to have more than one form of treatment. For example, talking with a therapist can help you deal with the effects of problems in your life, resolve conflict issues, and learn coping skills. And medication may help with chemical problems in the brain.

Even mild depression can lead to thoughts of suicide and suicide attempts. Many people have occasional thoughts of suicide when they are very upset, such as after breaking up with a boyfriend or girlfriend. But if you are feeling depressed and continue to think about hurting yourself and planning ways to end your life, you must tell someone and get professional help. If you won't tell an adult, tell a friend.

**ADD (or ADHD)** is another common mental health problem

among children and teens. Again, like depression, it's complicated. But the letters provide a pretty good clue: they stand for **A**ttention **D**eficit (**H**yperactivity) **D**isorder. That means you have a very hard time (much harder than most people) focusing on a single task or paying attention or staying still long enough to get something done. This problem is also often treated with medications.

**ODD** stands for Oppositional Defiant Disorder. It means that you are often defiant or hostile toward adults and sometimes your peers. And you often feel very angry and frustrated over things that don't seem to bother other people all that much. Of course, you may have good reasons to be angry. But if your anger is preventing you from being happy or working toward your goals (for example, because you're often getting disciplined at school, or taking illegal drugs to calm down), then you have a problem that you need to work on. ODD is typically treated in talk therapy and/or with medication.

**Anorexia** and **bulimia** are eating disorders. People who have **anorexia** become obsessed with getting rid of any fat on their body, and they eat less and less (and sometimes also exercise more and more). If they keep it up too long, they can actually starve to death. **Bulimia** is purposely throwing up your food before digesting it. Regularly throwing up food can cause its own health problems over time, like rotting teeth. And if the problem is related to anorexia, it can also contribute to starvation. Anorexia and bulimia are serious problems which require professional help and support.

**Self-mutilation** is when a person harms herself to create feelings of pain. A common form of self-mutilation is **cutting** where a person frequently cuts herself (or himself) to cause pain and bleeding. People who self-mutilate sometimes get pleasure or emotional release from pain, similar to what some people get from using drugs. Self-mutilation can cause physical problems such as scarring and infection. More importantly, it's a sign that something else is not right in your life. Therapy and even self-help groups can help you identify what's bothering you and begin to deal with the real problem.

**Substance abuse** means using drugs in ways that are harmful to you. You can abuse legal drugs (like caffeine, alcohol, cigarettes, and prescription medication, like Ritalin). Or you can abuse illegal drugs, like marijuana or cocaine. Substance abuse can be especially hard to deal with because some substances are addictive or strongly habit-forming, which makes quitting them very difficult. Regular use of some drugs can actually change your brain chemistry, so that it is harder for your brain to make the chemicals that naturally make you feel happy. Plus, using drugs usually makes it more difficult to think rationally, so it becomes harder to know that you have a problem.

### Kinds of Mental Health Professionals

**Psychologists** and **social workers** are trained mainly to do psychological counseling or therapy. That means they help with problems of feelings, relationships, habits, and behaviors. There are many different kinds of psychologists and social workers.

Some psychologists and social workers have extra training in very specialized areas, such as substance abuse, or teen issues, or working with whole families. If you have a specific problem, it may help to go to someone who has training or experience in those types of issues.

**Psychiatrists** are medical doctors with special training in mental health issues. In theory, that means they can help you with "talk therapy," just like psychologists and social workers. Psychiatrists are the ones who will prescribe medication when it is needed. If you are referred to a mental health center, you will probably be assigned to a therapist who is not a psychiatrist for talk therapy. If you and your therapist decide that you should consider medication, the psychiatrist's role will be to evaluate you by discussing your situation with you and your therapist, and prescribing the appropriate medication. The psychiatrist will continue to see you from time to time to evaluate your progress on the medication. As we said before, he or she will depend on you to report how the medication makes you feel so he or she can decide whether to continue with the same medication, change it, decrease or increase it, or discontinue it.

# Teens:
# How to Get More Out of This Book

*Self-help:* The teens who wrote the stories in this book did so because they hope that telling their stories will help readers who are facing similar challenges. They want you to know that you are not alone, and that taking specific steps can help you manage or overcome very difficult situations. They've done their best to be clear about the actions that worked for them so you can see if they'll work for you.

Our teen writers also helped put together the "Teen Guide to Getting Help" on p. 124. This guide explains what kind of help is out there for teens dealing with emotional problems, and how to get what you need.

**Resources on the Web**

We will occasionally post Think About It questions on our website, www.youthcomm.org, to accompany stories in this and other Youth Communication books. We try out the questions with teens and post the ones they like best. Many teens report that writing answers to those questions in a journal is very helpful.

# How to Use This Book in Staff Training

Staff say that reading these stories gives them greater insight into what teens are thinking and feeling, and new strategies for working with them. You can help the staff you work with by using these stories as case studies.

Select one story to read in the group, and ask staff to identify and discuss the main issue facing the teen. There may be disagreement about this, based on the background and experience of staff. That is fine. One point of the exercise is that teens have complex lives and needs. Adults can probably be more effective if they don't focus too narrowly and can see several dimensions of their clients.

Ask staff: What issues or feelings does the story provoke in them? What kind of help do they think the teen wants? What interventions are likely to be most promising? Least effective? Why? How would you build trust with the teen writer? How have other adults failed the teen, and how might that affect his or her willingness to accept help? What other resources would be helpful to this teen, such as peer support, a mentor, counseling, family therapy, etc.

**Resources on the Web**

From time to time we will post Think About It questions on our website, www.youthcomm.org, to accompany stories in this and other Youth Communication books. We try out the questions with teens and post the ones that they find most effective. We'll also post lesson for some of the stories. Adults can use the questions and lessons in workshops.

> **Discussion Guide**

# Teachers and Staff:
## How to Use This Book in Groups

When working with teens individually or in groups, using these stories can help young people face difficult issues in a way that feels safe to them. That's because talking about the issues in the stories usually feels safer to teens than talking about those same issues in their own lives. Addressing issues through the stories allows for some personal distance; they hit close to home, but not too close. Talking about them opens up a safe place for reflection. As teens gain confidence talking about the issues in the stories, they usually become more comfortable talking about those issues in their own lives.

Below are general questions that can help you lead discussions about the stories, which help teens and staff reflect on the issues in their own work and lives. In most cases you can read a story and conduct a discussion in one 45-minute session. Teens are usually happy to read the stories aloud, with each teen reading a paragraph or two. (Allow teens to pass if they don't want to read.) It takes 10-15 minutes to read a story straight through. However, it is often more effective to let workshop participants make comments and discuss the story as you go along. The workshop leader may even want to annotate her copy of the story beforehand with key questions.

If teens read the story ahead of time or silently, it's good to break the ice with a few questions that get everyone on the same page: Who is the main character? How old is she? What happened to her? How did she respond? Etc. Another good starting question is: "What stood out for you in the story?" Go around the room and let each person briefly mention one thing.

Then move on to open-ended questions, which encourage participants to think more deeply about what the writers were feeling, the choices they faced, and they actions they took. There are no right or wrong answers to the open-ended questions. Open-ended questions encourage participants to think about how the themes, emotions and choices in the stories relate to their own lives. Here are some examples of open-ended questions that we have found to be effective. You can use variations of these questions with almost any story in this book.

—What main problem or challenge did the writer face?

—What choices did the teen have in trying to deal with the problem?

—Which way of dealing with the problem was most effective for the teen? Why?

—What strengths, skills, or resources did the teen use to address the challenge?

—If you were in the writer's shoes, what would you have done?

—What could adults have done better to help this young person?

—What have you learned by reading this story that you didn't know before?

—What, if anything, will you do differently after reading this story?

—What surprised you in this story?

—Do you have a different view of this issue, or see a different way of dealing with it, after reading this story? Why or why not?

# Credits

The stories in this book originally appeared in the following Youth Communication publications:

"Don't Keep It Inside: Talk It Out," by Norman Brant, *Represent*, March/April 1998

"Therapy: What It's All About," by Carolyn Glaser, *Represent*, March/April 2001

"Getting Control Over My Moods," by Erica Harrigan, *Represent*, January/February 2006

"Get Outta My Head!" by Charlene Carter, *Represent*, March/April 2001

"Opening Up," by Natasha Santos, *Represent*, July/August 2007

"Getting Out of the Swamp," by Andrew Starr, *Represent*, July/August 2007

"My Journey Back from Depression," by Samira Hassan, *Represent*, July/August 1998

"Worried Sick," by Megan Cohen, *New Youth Connections*, September/October 2005

"Explaining Cognitive-Behavioral Therapy," by La'Quesha Barner, *Represent*, July/August 2007

"A Shy Girl Finds Her Voice," by Mayra Sierra, *Represent*, November/December 2003

"Listening to My Inner Child," by Aquellah Mahdi, *Represent*, September/October 2007

"Learning to Forgive," by Christopher B., *Represent*, March/April 1996

"Family Therapy: A Safe Place to Connect," *Represent*, September/October 2006

"Searching for Dr. Right," by Maya Noy, *Represent*, July/August 2007

"How Therapy Changed My Life," by Anonymous, *Represent*, November/December 1994

"A Hard Pill to Swallow," by Gloria Williams, *Represent*, March/April 2001

"What are Anti-Depressants?" by Carolyn Glaser, *Represent*, March/April 2001

"Inside a Psychiatrist's Head," by Gloria Williams, *Represent*, March/April, 2001

"Crazy for Psychology," by Erica Pierre, *New Youth Connections*, March 2007

"The Therapy Stigma," by Erica Pierre, *New Youth Connections*, March 2007

"Walking Away From the Fight," by Anonymous, *New Youth Connections*, January/February 2006

# About Youth Communication

Youth Communication, founded in 1980, is a nonprofit youth development program located in New York City whose mission is to teach writing, journalism, and leadership skills. The teenagers we train become writers for our websites and books and for two print magazines, *New Youth Connections*, a general-interest youth magazine, and *Represent*, a magazine by and for young people in foster care.

Each year, up to 100 young people participate in Youth Communication's school-year and summer journalism workshops where they work under the direction of full-time professional editors. Most are African American, Latino, or Asian, and many are recent immigrants. The opportunity to reach their peers with accurate portrayals of their lives and important self-help information motivates the young writers to create powerful stories.

Our goal is to run a strong youth development program in which teens produce high quality stories that inform and inspire their peers. Doing so requires us to be sensitive to the complicated lives and emotions of the teen participants while also providing an intellectually rigorous experience. We achieve that goal in the writing/teaching/editing relationship, which is the core of our program.

Our teaching and editorial process begins with discussions

between adult editors and the teen staff. In those meetings, the teens and the editors work together to identify the most important issues in the teens' lives and to figure out how those issues can be turned into stories that will resonate with teen readers.

Once story topics are chosen, students begin the process of crafting their stories. For a personal story, that means revisiting events in one's past to understand their significance for the future. For a commentary, it means developing a logical and persuasive point of view. For a reported story, it means gathering information through research and interviews. Students look inward and outward as they try to make sense of their experiences and the world around them and find the points of intersection between personal and social concerns. That process can take a few weeks or a few months. Stories frequently go through ten or more drafts as students work under the guidance of their editors, the way any professional writer does.

Many of the students who walk through our doors have uneven skills, as a result of poor education, living under extremely stressful conditions, or coming from homes where English is a second language. Yet, to complete their stories, students must successfully perform a wide range of activities, including writing and rewriting, reading, discussion, reflection, research, interviewing, and typing. They must work as members of a team and they must accept individual responsibility. They learn to provide constructive criticism, and to accept it. They engage in explorations of truthfulness, fairness, and accuracy. They meet deadlines. They must develop the audacity to believe that they have something important to say and the humility to recognize that saying it well is not a process of instant gratification. Rather, it usually requires a long, hard struggle through many discussions and much rewriting.

It would be impossible to teach these skills and dispositions as separate, disconnected topics, like grammar, ethics, or assertiveness. However, we find that students make rapid progress when they are learning skills in the context of an inquiry that is

## About Youth Communication

personally significant to them and that will benefit their peers.

When teens publish their stories—in *New Youth Connections* and *Represent,* on the web, and in other publications—they reach tens of thousands of teen and adult readers. Teachers, counselors, social workers, and other adults circulate the stories to young people in their classes and out-of-school youth programs. Adults tell us that teens in their programs—including many who are ordinarily resistant to reading—clamor for the stories. Teen readers report that the stories give them information they can't get anywhere else, and inspire them to reflect on their lives and open lines of communication with adults.

Writers usually participate in our program for one semester, though some stay much longer. Years later, many of them report that working here was a turning point in their lives—that it helped them acquire the confidence and skills that they needed for success in college and careers. Scores of our graduates have overcome tremendous obstacles to become journalists, writers, and novelists. They include National Book Award finalist Edwidge Danticat, novelist Ernesto Quinonez, writer Veronica Chambers and *New York Times* reporter Rachel Swarns. Hundreds more are working in law, business, and other careers. Many are teachers, principals, and youth workers, and several have started nonprofit youth programs themselves and work as mentors—helping another generation of young people develop their skills and find their voices.

---

*Youth Communication is a nonprofit educational corporation. Contributions are gratefully accepted and are tax deductible to the fullest extent of the law.*

*To make a contribution, or for information about our publications and programs, including our catalog of over 100 books and curricula for hard-to-reach teens, see www.youthcomm.org*

# About The Editors

**Laura Longhine** is the editorial director at Youth Communication, where she oversees editorial work on the organization's books, websites, and magazines. She edited *Represent*, Youth Communication's magazine by and for teens in foster care, for three years.

Prior to joining Youth Communication, Longhine was as a staff writer at the *Free Times*, an alt-weekly in South Carolina, and a freelance reporter for various publications. Her stories have been published in *The New York Times*, *Legal Affairs*, newyorkmetro.com, and *Child Welfare Watch*. She has a bachelor's in English from Tufts University and a master's in journalism from Columbia University.

Longhine is the editor of several other Youth Communication books, including *On The Move: Teens Write About Changing Placements* and *The Fury Inside: Teens Write About Anger*.

---

**Keith Hefner** co-founded Youth Communication in 1980 and has directed it ever since. He is the recipient of the Luther P. Jackson Education Award from the New York Association of Black Journalists and a MacArthur Fellowship. He was also a Revson Fellow at Columbia University.

# More Helpful Books
# From Youth Comunication

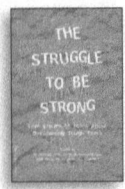
*The Struggle to Be Strong: True Stories by Teens About Overcoming Tough Times.* Foreword by Veronica Chambers. Help young people identify and build on their own strengths with 30 personal stories about resiliency. (Free Spirit)

*Fighting the Monster: Teens Write About Confronting Emotional Challenges and Getting Help.* Introduction by Dr. Francine Cournos. Teens write about their struggle to achieve emotional well-being. Topics include: Cutting, depression, bereavement, substance abuse, and more. (Youth Communication)

*Depression, Anger, Sadness: Teens Write About Facing Difficult Emotions.* Give teens the confidence they need to seek help when they need it. These teens write candidly about difficult emotional problems—such as depression, cutting, and domestic violence—and how they have tried to help themselves. (Youth Communication)

*My Secret Addiction: Teens Write About Cutting.* These true accounts of cutting, or self-mutilation, offer a window into the personal and family situations that lead to this secret habit, and show how teens can get the help they need. (Youth Communication)

*Enjoy the Moment: Teens Write About Dealing With Stress.* Help decrease the levels of stress and conflict in your teens' lives. These young writers describe how they cope with stress, using methods including meditation, journal writing, and exercise. (Youth Communication)

 *The Fury Inside: Teens Write About Anger.* Help teens manage their anger. These writers tell how they got better control of their emotions and sought the support of others. (Youth Communication)

*Out of the Shadows: Teens Write About Surviving Sexual Abuse.* Help teens feel less alone and more hopeful about overcoming the trauma of sexual abuse. This collection includes first-person accounts by male and female survivors grappling with fear, shame, and guilt. (Youth Communication)

 *Putting the Pieces Together Again: Teens Write About Surviving Rape.* These stories show how teens have coped with the nightmare experience of rape and taken steps toward recovery. (Youth Communication)

*Sticks and Stones: Teens Write About Bullying.* Shed light on bullying, as told from the perspectives of the bully, the victim, and the witness. These stories show why bullying occurs, the harm it causes, and how it might be prevented. (Youth Communication)

 *Out With It: Gay and Straight Teens Write About Homosexuality.* Break stereotypes and provide support with this unflinching look at gay life from a teen's perspective. With a focus on urban youth, this book also includes several heterosexual teens' transformative experiences with gay peers. (Youth Communication)

---

*To order these and other books, go to:*
**www.youthcomm.org**
*or call 212-279-0708 x115*

www.ingramcontent.com/pod-product-compliance
Lightning Source LLC
Chambersburg PA
CBHW071725090426
42738CB00009B/1887